Envisioning Knowledge

Building Literacy in the Academic Disciplines

Judith A. Langer

Teachers College, Columbia University
New York and London

KH

Published by Teachers College Press, 1234 Amsterdam Avenue, New York, NY 10027

Library of Congress Cataloging-in-Publication Data

Langer, Judith A.
  Envisioning knowledge : building literacy in the academic disciplines / Judith A. Langer.
       p. cm.—(Language and literacy series)
  Includes bibliographical references and index.
  ISBN 978-0-8077-5158-9 (pbk. : alk. paper)
  ISBN 978-0-8077-5159-6 (hardcover : alk. paper)
    1. Literacy—Study and teaching. 2. Information literacy—Study and teaching. 3. Critical pedagogy. I. Title.
  LC149.L225   2011
  428.0071—dc22   2010026441

ISBN 978-0-8077-5158-9 (paper)
ISBN 978-0-8077-5159-6 (hardcover)

Printed on acid-free paper
Manufactured in the United States of America

18 17 16 15 14 13 12 11   8 7 6 5 4 3 2 1

2/28/12

*This book is dedicated
to my granddaughters*

Eliana and Gavriela,

*whose words and thoughts
enliven Chapter 1,
and whose voices are the voices
of our future.*

Contents

Preface   **xi**

1. Envisioning Knowledge: An Introduction   **1**
Academic Literacy   2
The Growth of Academic Literacy   3
Why Academic Literacy Matters   11
Literate Thinking and Gaining Knowledge   12
Summing Up   14

2. The Origins of Envisionment Building   **16**
Envisionment Building   16
Stances During Envisionment Building   21
The Stances as an Instructional Tool   23
Summing Up   27

3. How We Build Literate Knowledge   **28**
Orientations Toward Meaning   28
How the Orientations Affect Instruction   30
How the Orientations Relate to One Another   32
Fostering Both Orientations in Disciplinary Classes   36
Summing Up   38

4. Envisionment-Building Classrooms   **39**
What Envisionment-Building Classrooms Look Like   41
Features of Minds-On Teaching   43
The Individual Within the Group   51
Summing Up   51

5. **Envisionment Building in Social Studies/History**   **53**

   Instructional Foci in Social Studies/History   55

   A Minds-On Social Studies/History Class   57

   Using the Stances in 8th-Grade Social
   Studies/History Special Education   67

   Online Discussion in a High School World History Class   73

   Summing Up   75

6. **Envisionment Building in Science**   **77**

   What and How Scientists Know   78

   An 8th-Grade Science Class:
   Sustained Discussion and Writing About Experiments   80

   Thinking Critically in a High School Physics Class   88

   Summing Up   90

7. **Envisionment Building in Mathematics**   **92**

   Learning Mathematics by Engaging in Applied Activities   92

   Sustained Discussion and Problem Solving
   for 12th-Grade Struggling Mathematicians   94

   An 8th-Grade Class Developing
   Math Concepts Through Problem-Based Activities   103

   Summing Up   112

8. **Envisionment Building in English**   **114**

   Thinking with and Through Language   114

   Cognitive and Linguistic Aspects of English Learning   115

   How a 9th-Grade English Class
   Explores Vocabulary and Content   117

   Making Literary Comparisons in 12th-Grade English   121

   Online Research in a Special Education Class   126

   Summing Up   130

9. **Envisionment Building Across Disciplines:
   Teachers Collaborating in a Professional Community**   **131**

   Coming Together   134

   Year 1: Developing Problem-Based, Minds-On Activities   135

Year 2: Enhancing Critical Thinking Through Writing 137
Year 3: Learning and Thinking More Deeply in the Disciplines 148
Continuing Self-Study 151
Summing Up 153

10. Closing the Circle:
   The Role of Literacy in Disciplinary Knowledge **155**
   Constructive Envisionment Building 155
   Building Knowledge and Gaining Higher Literacy 156
   Technology as a Cognitive Playground for Disciplinary Literacy 158
   Summing Up 158

References **161**

Index **167**

About the Author **175**

Preface

This book is long overdue. It was conceived during the late 1990s and has been germinating ever since. Then, as now, we needed to rethink how one gains knowledge and becomes literate within the academic areas. What does it mean to gain disciplinary literacy—to be able to understand and communicate in ways that mark "knowing" within a field? In educational research and theory, there is a long-standing body of work that looks at the content of specific school subjects to answer this question. However, much research, including mine, suggests that it isn't merely the content but also the ways of thinking about it that are at the heart of learning.

Although this book features new studies conducted within the past 10 years, it builds on my earlier research. In 1987–1988, I conducted a series of studies that were very important at the time, and still are. They examined the ways in which people, adults as well as students, went about constructing understandings of various literary and informational texts. In one study, for example, students were asked to think aloud as they read poems and stories, as well as science and social studies/history texts of various sorts. I also looked at classrooms in all four of the core subjects (English, math, science, and social studies/history), finding differences in the kinds of thinking in which students were engaged, as well as the kinds of teaching they were experiencing.

Less formally, I also looked at how adults participated in book groups and paid attention to the conversations people had as they left movie theaters—again looking for differences in how they made sense of what they had experienced. My concerns grew from three different sources. First, during the mid-1980s, I had completed a study looking at the ways in which high school and college teachers talked about "knowing" their subjects, and what that meant for their teaching. Surprisingly, many were uncomfortable with engaging their students in writing or discussion, although a number of studies had shown that both writing and discussion are useful tools to deepen content learning. Second, as a

long-term consultant for the National Assessment of Educational Progress (NAEP), I knew that students' abilities to think deeply about the
material they were reading and writing about had made little progress
over time, despite many efforts to improve instruction. Lastly, I had long
been concerned that, although the field of education had developed
ways to think and talk about scientific and mathematical reasoning, we
had no similar constructs for discussing literary reasoning—despite the
fact that literature had always been and continues to be the core content
of English classes.

My 1987–1988 studies indicated that there are consistently different
ways in which people go about constructing understandings based upon
whether their goal is to gain information or to engage in a literary experience. I was also able to specify these differences, which I discuss in the
early chapters of this book. This led me into a long series of studies that
focused on making sense of literature, when the primary purpose is to
engage in a literary experience—to step into the text like we all do when
we curl up with a novel of our own choice. I felt that these studies were
critical because so little had been written on the subject and the roles of
literary thinking and literature instruction had been largely ignored. I set
out to develop a pedagogy designed to help students become more expert
literary thinkers—the basis of my book *Envisioning Literature*.

As time went on, I realized that I still needed to get back to the other
half of the work I had begun—to study, develop, and specify a pedagogy
for ways in which students could come to think more deeply and learn
more fully in their other subjects. Over the past 10 years, through a series
of studies and instructional development projects, I developed a framework designed to guide students to understand more deeply and become
more highly literate within a range of disciplines, drawing on expository
as well as literary orientations. Thus, this book was born.

In the first four chapters of this book, I explain how one thinks during content learning, and how one comes to know. Using my studies
in middle and secondary schools as a backdrop, Chapters 5–8 focus on
"envisionment-building" classrooms-in-action, demonstrating how students gain knowledge and the ways in which they can most effectively
be taught in each of the core subjects. I also demonstrate ways in which
critical thinking through reading, writing, and discussion contributes to
knowledge building and how these processes can help students learn the
particular disciplinary content, language, and ways of reasoning that are
valued within each field. I use Chapter 9 to portray an interdisciplinary

team of teachers embracing the features discussed in the previous chapters, as they plan, make curricular decisions, and develop a collaborative professional community over time. In closing, Chapter 10 revisits and then goes beyond the role of literacy in disciplinary knowledge in both school classrooms and students' lives.

Overall, I offer a framework for conceptualizing envisionment building in the various academic subjects, and ways this framework can undergird successful practices across the curriculum—practices that help students do better not only in their coursework, but on their high-stakes exams and in their lives as well.

Envisioning Knowledge calls on the Partnership for Literacy intervention study I co-directed with Arthur Applebee and Martin Nystrand, as well as my own follow-up research and development projects across subject areas and across grades in more than 40 schools as a source of theory and practice. Because I have had the good fortune to have collaborated with highly generous, professional, and excellent teachers in a range of localities with a range of students, the chapters that follow provide abundant and rich classroom examples from social studies/history, science, mathematics, and English.

The various projects on which this book is based could never have been completed without the professional interest and personal dedication of the administrators, teachers, and students in the schools in which we worked. Although most remain anonymous in this book, I thank each of them deeply, and hope all I have learned from them can serve in some small measure as repayment for their generous contributions. In the course of your reading, you will come across many names. The first time I mention them in any chapter, I have placed an asterisk next to those who have been given a pseudonym and who will remain anonymous. All other teachers, those whose names are left untouched in their first occurrence in a chapter, have been kind enough to permit me to use their real names. All student and school names are pseudonyms.

I owe a great debt to the instructional facilitators, Kathy Nickson, Eija Rougle, Johanna Shogan, and Karen Polsinelli, for their hard work and expertise. Johanna and Karen were project teachers when we began, but, to our good fortune, they later joined our Partnership for Literacy team. It is through the entire team that I continue to learn. Because Eija Rougle has worked with me since about 1990, on so many of my research projects, she has become one of my closest collaborators. I can't thank her enough for her enormous assistance in the development of this book. Since sometime in the 1990s, Janet Angelis has been director of outreach and later associate director of the Center for English Learning & Achievement (CELA) and the Albany Institute for Research in Education (AIRE), both of which I direct. Among her many leadership roles has been her admirable oversight of the Partnership for Literacy's development program. I send warm thanks to her for her generous colleagueship and help across these many years. I am grateful to my colleagues who provided helpful guidance to my subject-specific queries along the way, especially Sam Wineburg, Vicky Kouba, Carmel Shettino, and Alandeom Oliveira. Meg Lemke, my editor at Teachers College Press, has been most supportive and a delight to work with. My deepest thanks go to my closest collaborator and most constant sounding board, Arthur Applebee, whose brief comments and grimaces are appreciated more than he ever imagines.

J.A.L.
New York City

CHAPTER 1

Envisioning Knowledge:
An Introduction

What is knowledge? How do we gain it? How do we teach it? These are important questions, because knowledge is not merely a compilation of facts about a topic. It includes understanding how these facts interrelate with one another, how they interrelate with other knowledge, and what belongs (as well as what doesn't belong) in that construct. Knowledge is crafted and honed. It requires an understanding of social and disciplinary conventions surrounding the ideas. What we think about, and the ways we think when we build an understanding, bolster an argument, create a proof, analyze data, or offer evidence, differ across cultures and social groups and differ from discipline to discipline.

For example, before we can say we really know someone, we need to learn a lot about that person. We need to know about the individual's family, educational, religious, and social backgrounds; likes and dislikes; life story; work; and current views. Then we need to connect information we already have in ways that build an image of a whole person, one we can check against past or future input.

Like knowing someone, all knowledge is relational and requires an active and probing mind, as well as a mind that already knows something about the content, context, and conventions. For example, in social studies/history, we use data from a variety of perspectives (including temporal, social, historical, economic, political, and geographic) to explain by instantiating ourselves in time, through contextualization of similarities and contrasts, or by questioning authors' viewpoints. In biology, where systems and their functions are so important, we use data about functions within the larger system to explain and describe systems of classification. In physics, on the other hand, where observations of natural phenomena are central, we examine possible explanations of observed phenomena and relate them to accepted principles of physics. In literature, we arrive at interpretations by exploring multiple perspectives from within and outside the text, and consider possible implications through analysis of the text itself, as well as its relationship to other texts, literary theories, and life. Here, we use the text, relevant knowledge, and personal experience as substantiating data. (See Langer 1992a, 1992b, 1994 for more about these disciplinary descriptions.)

Each field involves multiple acts of knowledge building as we seek data and use them to go beyond the information given in ways that are appropriate to the field. In this sense, knowledge is much deeper than simply getting information. Information counts, of course, but what you do with it and to what end creates knowledge. Disciplinary traditions and conventions need to be understood, even as new generations try to break from and extend them.

ACADEMIC LITERACY

In this book, I will limit my discussion to academic literacy—the kind we learn at school, in middle and high school courses: English, mathematics, science, and social studies/history. How do we learn to build academic literacy? Life experiences get us started; school experiences pull us in even further. Through informational experiences—be they oral, written, electronic, or kinesthetic, or in modes of presentation not yet invented—people learn to focus on a topic, to narrow in on what is relevant as they search for and consider ideas and evidence pertaining to that topic. They make judgments about what is critical to weave together a conceptual construct that they can fine-tune, build upon, or even disagree with at a later time. Through this process of focusing, narrowing, searching, considering, questioning, judging, tuning, and rejecting, they learn not merely to receive knowledge, but to own it. They make sense. And if they probe deeply enough and connect wisely enough, they create knowledge. That knowledge is theirs, available to them for whatever purposes they wish in whatever experiences they encounter. If they are students, they become the literate thinkers we need to shape the knowledge and world of tomorrow—young people who think clearly and learn well. They can seek answers, ask probing questions about things as they are, and construct new ideas and paradigms.

Disciplinary Thought and Language

To engage in academic literacy we must learn to select and control the aspects of disciplinary thought and language that serve as markers, ones that carry meaning and are widely understood and used within a discipline. These markers denote the social conventions that are subject- or context-specific, those that people within that field know, understand, and expect others "in the know" to use. Using these disciplinary markers of literacy and understanding, and knowing what they mean when others use them, fosters a sense of belonging within a discipline and contributes to the confidence a learner needs in order to explore and question ideas that go beyond the given. It permits individuals to understand the oral and written texts they encounter more deeply and helps them connect and build larger constructs, question faulty ones, hone their thinking within the field, and connect and use their knowledge across disciplines and life contexts.

This is the kind of academic literacy that can underlie reading, writing, discussion, media use, and activities in all school subjects. It is at the heart of gaining knowledge in disciplines and can be at the heart of teaching and learning in every subject-area classroom. It is the kind of literacy that empowers all students, whoever they are and whatever they have experienced, to participate in the specific language and ways of thinking particular to a discipline.

THE GROWTH OF ACADEMIC LITERACY

Some people feel that students, particularly younger ones and poorly performing ones, are unable to engage in the use of academic language and thought until they are taught the building blocks. In particular, there is an assumption in child development that narrative talk precedes exposition (informational talk), that it is easier to do. However, research in child language has indicated that children at an early, preschool age move beyond narrative as a matter of course, and some studies have demonstrated that the expository form can appear first (e.g., Beals & Snow, 1994; Bissex, 1980; Liberg, Espmark, Wiksten, & Butler, 1997; Pappas, 1991; Zecker, 1996). In one of my own studies of the language features that 8-, 11-, and 14-year-olds use when they read and write (Langer, 1985, 1986a), I found that students as young as 3rd grade have a good sense of both narrative and expository structures. However, the expository forms they know differ from those used in academic situations; some new essential structures need to be introduced and acquired through more "school learning." It is my conviction that reading, writing, and familiarity with language, structure, and disciplinary conventions are at the root of learning in academic coursework. They need to be taught, through first-hand disciplinary experience, as language and thought-in-use, in content-area classes.

From Home to School

Although this book is about middle and high school disciplines, I will begin with a much younger example to demonstrate that aspects of academic genres—what to think about and say and how to structure the talk—are learned quite early, within the context of daily life. Building from that, the more sophisticated forms that children need for disciplinary learning can continue to be learned at school, in the context of daily school life from the early grades onward. There is a trajectory into which teachers must hook. Let's look at some examples.

From the stages of early literacy, as early as the second year of life, children unearth the most wonderful distinctions between literary and informational thought and language. We see this in the content and structure of their communications. Here is Gavriela, from a middle-class family with college-educated parents. At 2 years, 11 months, she is engaged in dramatic play with Awilda, her babysitter. Notice her use of dialogue to move the story along.

> *Gavriela*: Let's play doctor.
> *Awilda*: Who's the doctor?
> *Gavriela*: You're the doctor.
> *Awilda*: And you're the patient?
> *Gavriela*: Yes.
> *Awilda*: Hello, Miss Patient. Can I help you?
> *Gavriela*: Meow, meow.
> *Awilda*: Hi, Miss Kitty Cat. Are you sick, or something bothering you today?
> *Gavriela*: Meow. (Points to her stomach)
> *Awilda*: Your tummy. What did you eat today?

> *Gavriela*: A lot of stuff. Macaroni. Cheese. Cereal.
> *Awilda*: What can I give you for it? Maybe a teaspoon of medicine.
>   I'll pour it into a spoon.
> *Gavriela*: Okay.
> *Awilda*: Here we go. That should make the kitty's tummy feel better.
> *Gavriela*: (Pointing to the make-believe bottle) Now close it up.
> *Awilda*: How are you feeling now?
> *Gavriela*: Good.
> *Awilda*: I'll see you later.
> *Gavriela*: (Curls into a chair to take a make-believe nap) I feel better
>   now.

Gavriela is making believe, and uses her first words to move both herself and her babysitter into a story world. Instead of saying, "Once upon a time," she says, "Let's play doctor." These serve the same purpose, to signal an imaginative experience, and both participants adjust their language to engage in it. In fact, Gavriela overtly demands that they maintain this story (or literary) orientation by reminding Awilda to close the make-believe medicine bottle.

She becomes a cat; by using the cat's voice and action, Gavriela maintains a story orientation throughout this scenario. She is always the cat, and she holds Awilda to her role as the doctor. Further, Gavriela's story has a beginning, middle, and end—a happy ending at that, when as the make-believe cat, she declares that she is feeling better.

Now, let us look briefly at Gavriela's use of expository thought and language. Here, at 2 years and 7 months, she recounts a trip that she and her family had taken to a historic restoration in Wisconsin. She is giving information.

> Once my mom and dad and my sister and me went camping. We
> went into a house. We went inside. We went upstairs. There wasn't
> anything there. No, there were sheep and horses.

This recount took place 4 months earlier than her cat story. (My use here of the word *recount* comes from Liberg, Epsmark, Wiksten, and Butler, 1997.) Gavriela knows that she must retell her experience in a time sequence, with details. And she appropriately maintains this structure throughout. Further, she also knows the kind of content that must accompany a recount. She knows the rules of journalistic exposition, telling who, what, when, and where. She is brief and tries to be accurate with her details, even correcting herself when needed. When we compare the two, we can see that she knows about genre differences—that she knows the sorts of content, language, and structures that are appropriate for each genre.

Next is a sample of Gavriela's expository retelling of what she learned in science, about the moon. It was told during the spring of her kindergarten year.

> The moon is soft, so your footprints show. A full moon is actually only half of the moon. The other part is hidden. When you are on the moon, you can see that it is bigger than it seems from here. The moon does not need its own light. The sunlight bounces off the moon and makes it light for the moon. ([As an aside, looking up with a twinkle in her eye] The sun and the moon must be best friends.) Maybe the moon is soft because the sun melts the top of the moon. This could also not be true.

We can see that she has been selective about what she chooses to share, focusing on important information she learned about the moon. She knows her jokes are not part of the genre for presenting science information, and therefore uses nonverbal cues to show the listener that she means it as an aside. But then she goes beyond simply telling the most important things she learned, by using her knowledge to ask questions that might take her beyond what she already knows. She has heard that the moon is soft, and is curious why this might be so. She uses her knowledge of the effects of the sun's heat on some substances and makes a conjecture. However, she knows she does not yet possess enough information about the moon's surface to be certain. Thus, she has created a subtopic about the moon to pursue at some later time. We can see that her science lessons at school have given her more than critical information about the moon; they have also introduced her to a language, structure, and way of thinking that is particularly appropriate for science.

At the end of her year in kindergarten, Gavriela's teacher gave the class some work to do during the summer. One written assignment was: "Make up a story about butterflies that has a take-away number." This is what Gavriela wrote in her journal (with some help with spelling and letter orientation):

I went to the park. I saw 8 butterflies. When I turned to look at the flowers, two of them had flown away. How many are left?

Then she did the calculation (using her fingers) and said as she wrote, "6."

Thus, by the end of her kindergarten year, Gavriela already had enough experience of different school subjects to know the difference between a literary story and a mathematics story. Although they both have an element of make-believe, the language and structures are quite different, as are their purposes. Beyond this, her ability to use her own language to create a word problem that she then could answer indicates that she understands the underlying structure of a math problem, an understanding that should hold her in good stead as these problems become more complex in her math classes across the school years.

Zoom ahead once again, and we see that by the end of 1st grade she is already able to write a book report, after having devoured the book on her own (see Figure 1.1). In this example, we see that she knows the

Figure 1.1. Gavriela's Book Report

Gavriela's   Reading Reviews

I just finished reading Liberty Porter first Daughter
by Julia Devillers

It's about a girl who's the President's daughter

In the beginning, her family is moving into the White House! She's getting used to it... sort of.

Then, She learns there are many places she can't go in the White House!

At the end, she has lots of fun. She even gets a smile out of Mrs. Gump.

The part I liked best is when she dresses as a boy and helps people out.

I do do not recommend this book for children my age because it's so funny. I love it. It's a great book.

content that is appropriate to write about and can place it into a simple beginning/middle/end report structure. She knows how to use capitals and lowercase letters (almost always), contractions, and even voice (e.g., when she uses "sort of"). She also knows how to write an introductory sentence and an evaluative ending. In fact, at this point in her development she can give a report using this structure without the story-starter scaffold. She is ready to move on to more complex reports that contain elements such as elaborations, explanations, and evidence.

Clearly, the conventions of language, structure, and content that Gavriela began to learn at home were appropriate for the kind of recounting that families do after an outing or other experience. She learned them in the usual context of her daily family life and interactions. And when she began kindergarten, she was exposed to "school talk"—the various academic disciplines, what they talk about, and how. Her experiences with academic language and structure continued through 1st grade and will continue to grow throughout her years at school. Such conventions are exceedingly useful in her learning of subject-matter content, as well as in how she thinks about it. They help her gain expectations about what she is to do cognitively: what kind of information to look for and what to do with it in the context of specific academic disciplines. She has begun on her path to academic literacy.

During the School Years

Now let's fast-forward to an adolescent. We'll begin with a lab report that Gavriela's then-12-year-old sister Eliana did for her science class. It was called the Rock Shake Experiment, and Figure 1.2 shows what Eliana wrote.

Eliana did this experiment in November of 7th grade. By that time, she clearly had learned not merely the format and language of lab reports, but also the ways of thinking about experiments, their procedures and outcomes, that are appropriate for her science class. She also added a new disciplinary word related to this unit to her usable vocabulary, *abrasion*. Although her hypothesis was not substantiated by her experiment, it is likely she could have run some further tests to examine her conclusion.

Now, look below at selections from a four-page paper, written and edited on a computer, assigned as part of a unit on the Constitution for Eliana's 8th-grade social studies/history class. She received an A– for it. You will see that some features of academic literacy that she would have

Figure 1.2. Eliana's Rock Shake Experiment

Hypothesis:

> If limestone is exposed to water, the mass of the limestone will lower a little.
>
> If limestone is exposed to vinegar, the mass of the limestone will lower a little.
>
> If limestone is exposed to shaking, the mass of the limestone will lower a little.

Data and Observations:

Container	Total Mass (g) Day 1	Total Mass (g) Day 2	Change in Mass (g)	% Change in Mass
A (water, no shaking)	17g	17.1g	1g	.6%
B (water, shaking)	15.2g	15.2g	0g	0%
C (vinegar, no shaking)	15g	14.6g	.4g	2.7%
D (vinegar, shaking)	11.6g	8.5g	3.1g	26.7%

Analysis:

Change in mass: 11.6 - 8.5 = 3.1

$\qquad\qquad$ 15 - 14.6 = .4

Percent change in mass: 3.1 × 100/11.6 = 26.7

$\qquad\qquad\qquad\qquad$ .4 x 100/15 = 2.7

Results:

Variable Tested	Effects of variable tested on mass of limestone:
Water	Raises the mass a little bit
Vinegar	Creates a lot of pressure that expands the bottle, has gas, lowers the mass, smells bad
Shaking	Lowers the mass, creates a lot of bubbles (mainly in vinegar), causes the rock to break into pieces (abrasion)

Conclusion:

My hypothesis for water was incorrect, but I think that the limestone's mass could have stayed the same.

learned 7 years earlier, when she was Gavriela's age, continue to be appropriate, while others have been added.

In 1777, a group of delegates from the United States of America sat down to write a constitution for the newborn nation. They came out with the Articles of Confederation, a document that proved to be weak and one that did not work at all. To keep from having an all-powerful central government the delegates had given most of the power to the states. The national government had to beg the states for essential things such as money, because it did not have the power to tax the people directly, and soldiers, because it could not enlist its own. Each state had its own currency not valid in any other state. The national government could not regulate interstate trade, so all the states were fighting over boundaries, and taxing each other just to travel between the states. The national government was deep in debt, and had to ask the states for money often not granted. Something needed to change. In May 1787, another group of delegates was asked to meet in Philadelphia to look at and revise the Articles of the Confederation. . . .

The writers of the Constitution were greatly influenced by a French writer named Montesquieu. One of his ideas that they used was separation of powers. It is a system of government where they have three different branches. . . .

The writers of the constitution used another idea of Montesquieu's. This was the idea of checks and balances. . . .

Federalism is another hugely important part of the Constitution. . . .

The Bill of Rights is the first 10 amendments to the Constitution. . . .

The writers of the Constitution needed to create a government that was strong, but was not authoritarian, and most importantly, that it would last. . . . The writers most definitely proved that without England's rule, we were a stronger country, and inspired many people around the world.

In addition to narrowing in on her topic, the Constitution, Eliana's knowledge was broad enough for her to divide her paper into six paragraphs, each focusing on a separate subtopic related to the Constitution. In the full paper, she displays her knowledge of social studies/ history thinking by making her points within the context of that era and then providing substantiating data. She makes connections and explains why the Articles of Confederation didn't work and why the Constitution did. To do this, she uses a social studies/history form of argumentation, where social, political, and economic issues examined in context are brought to bear.

She opens her paper with a background introduction and thesis. The next four paragraphs focus on the separation of powers, checks and balances, federalism, and the Bill of Rights. Her last paragraph serves as her conclusion. Just as Gavriela showed that she had been gaining the early stages of academic literacy, Eliana is a good example of a young adolescent who is quite comfortable with the social studies and science disciplines and their special conventions of language and thought. We can expect her academic literacy to continue to grow as she moves into high school.

WHY ACADEMIC LITERACY MATTERS

In this book, I will show how engagement in the thought and language of middle and high school academic courses helps students of all levels of school success learn two very important aspects of academic literacy:

1. The course content set in relevant context and its connection to larger constructs within the course, the field, other fields, and the world
2. The ways of thinking and the language and structures that are used and valued by the discipline in conveying these ideas

My studies indicate that all students can enter these worlds of academic literacy. Once they do, their understanding of the concepts and ability to use and communicate them can grow across the years—as in the examples above.

Further, I will argue, this sort of academic literacy is best taught and learned within each discipline. It is by participating in classes where students and their teachers engage in activities that are appropriate to the discipline that disciplinary ideas can be tried out, supported, and learned. It is in these disciplinary contexts that knowledge can be sharpened and extended and where academic literacy, as well as new ideas, can grow. Both the knowledge and the ways of thinking about it are then available to be used in flexible ways as they appear in use across disciplines, or are called upon in creating new cross-disciplinary connections.

Before I describe these classrooms, I want to introduce a core concept that reverberates throughout the rest of this book—literate thinking.

LITERATE THINKING AND GAINING KNOWLEDGE

When people talk about literacy, they are generally referring to reading and writing, but to me it means much more. To convey what I mean, I have found it useful to talk about *literate thinking*. I first developed this concept in the early 1980s when I was trying to understand the ways in which people gain literacy within particular eras, cultures, and circumstances (e.g., see Langer 1987, 1995). It is one of the concepts that has grown over time and become an essential part of my understanding of literacy.

This concept extends beyond the acts of reading and writing themselves to include what we think about and do when we gain knowledge, reason with it, and communicate about it in a variety of contexts—at home, at school, on the job, and in the rest of our lives—even when we are not reading or writing. There are some common abilities we call upon when we read, write, think, and speak—when we use the various signs, languages, dialects, and technologies that bring and convey meaning (e.g., Kress, Jewitt, Franks, Hardcastle, Jones, & Bourne 2005; Morris, 1971; Peirce, 1992; Sebeok & Danesi, 2000).

From this perspective, we can think of literacy as the ability to think like a literate person, to call upon the kinds of reasoning abilities that people generally use when they read and write (such as the ability to reflect on text, symbols, and their meanings), even when reading and writing are not involved, and even in the context of electronic or graphic modes and media. Here, the focus is not just on the reading and writing, but also on the thinking that accompanies it. From this perspective, literacy happens when certain kinds of thinking take place, whatever the technology used.

It is a given that new knowledge-building technologies that serve as tools for thought will continue to be invented. Therefore, my notion of literacy accounts for them, even before I know what they might be, because by definition they will continue or extend our uses of literate thinking. Literate thinking can take place around any set of signs and symbols within a society (e.g., Flood, Lapp, Brice-Heath, & Langer, 2009). Environment, culture, and experience are all implicated in the different kinds of interpretations and meanings these might bring. Who we are and what we have experienced have a strong influence on the meanings we develop, as well as on our reactions to the experience.

Literate thinking refers to the skills and strategies we use to gain meaning and build knowledge from any and all these modes of input, whoever we are and whatever meanings we develop. If we have interpretations that are different from others, it is not because we didn't engage in literate thinking, but because certain factors led us to *this* rather than *that* understanding. Our options are to question others' understandings, seek explanations and challenges, and weigh the evidence. We need to use literate thinking to stretch others' as well as our own ideas, to realize that our own or others' ideas could not adequately be defended and need to be dropped, or to accept that there may be more than one way to look at things and try to understand the various perspectives.

For example, suppose you had read the best-selling book *Dreams from My Father* by Barack Obama (1995) because you knew that he was a presidential candidate and you wanted to get a fuller sense of him as a person. While reading the book, you searched for passages that foretold or seemed related to some of Obama's campaign positions, to get a sense of the depth and longevity of his convictions and to see how his past might have inspired him to argue for new actions for new times. You then might have analyzed the relevant portions of the book, compared them with his actions, and discussed your ideas with friends and colleagues, reacting to their points and adding some of your own. I think all of us would have considered this an act of literacy.

Now, suppose you had seen the movie *Frost/Nixon*, about David Frost's interviews of ex-President Richard Nixon after he had been impeached. You had previously heard about the Watergate cover-up and how duplicitous acts contributed to public mistrust of government, beyond Watergate itself. While watching the movie, you searched for instances of words or behavior and analyzed them in their context, then compared them to see if they had any relevance for the present time. Then you discussed your ideas with your friends and colleagues, reacted to their points, and added some of your own. From my perspective, this, too, is an act of literacy.

The book and the film evoke similar cognitive skills and strategies; whether reading or writing took place or not, the thinking did. And it is these kinds of thinking that lie at the heart of literate behavior and permit us to think purposefully and deeply, and to gain, weigh, and sharpen our knowledge.

Although the examples I have given come from my own life and experiences, they could easily have taken place in an American history class where issues of ethics and moral responsibility are examined from the perspective of the presidential office. Surely, students' interpretations might differ. We would expect differences of interpretation and opinion, followed by discussion and debate involving argument and evidence to ensue. With guidance, this could involve the teaching and learning of academic literacy. The meanings we gain from literate thinking are situation-based and dependent upon the individuals involved. Therefore, experience, culture, and society's expectations, as well as the values and conventions within a particular discipline, all affect the different kinds of interpretations and meanings that people might develop. Of course, gender, race, class, disabilities, and related aspects of a person's background affect the meanings we develop, as well as how we interpret and use our knowledge. Thus we need to inspect and understand our own perspectives as well as others' and to question and probe beneath the surface. Subject-area teachers, who are disciplinary experts, need to guide, model, and provide opportunities for students to try out and step into the ways of thinking that are appropriate to that discipline. They can give students a chance to use disciplinary language and thought in ways that help them refine their understandings and gain knowledge. Teachers can help students become literate thinkers in the various academic disciplines.

SUMMING UP

I believe the concept of literate thinking I have presented can take us much further in developing new visions of successful academic literacy than simply focusing on the acts of reading and writing. Literate thinking begins when we are very young, even younger than Gavriela; is honed at school in our subject-area classes; grows with us; enables us; and opens routes of knowledge for us to use throughout our lives. It helps our ideas develop; our questioning, probing, and crafting help our knowledge to grow. To gain knowledge, we build envisionments. This will be the focus of the next chapter.

CHAPTER 2

The Origins of Envisionment Building

Those of us who have special interests or knowledge we would like to share with others, those of us who are interested in how the mind works when learning, and those of us who are now or who aspire to become teachers have some very basic questions we need to ask ourselves:

- What is learning?
- How can I help it happen?
- How can I know it has happened?

The first is the critical question from which the other two follow. From what I have already discussed in the first chapter, you can see that I think learning involves active and inquiring minds being engaged in discipline-appropriate experiences. I also think the uses of language, and the ways of thinking that permit ideas to be generated, need to be tried out and learned in a content-rich environment. Embedded experiences are critical, because through them learners come to understand the words and structures of the discipline and to contextualize new topics within a larger universe of meaning and action—in whatever medium or technology they use. When students engage in substantive content-embedded experiences over time, they gain discipline-specific knowledge. I see this process occurring through the act of envisionment building.

ENVISIONMENT BUILDING

What are envisionments? In the last chapter and the introduction to this one, I began to describe the knowledge-building experience. Knowledge grows from a person's desire to make sense, in class or in the world outside. It is an active quest that takes time, experience, and many acts of envisionment building. Envisionments[1] are the worlds of knowledge in our minds that are made up of what we understand and what we don't about a particular topic or experience at any point in time. They are dynamic sets of related ideas, questions, images, anticipations, agreements, arguments, and hunches that fill our minds during every reading, writing, discussion, technology interaction, or other experience where we gain or express thoughts and understandings. Each envisionment includes what we do or do not understand, as well as any momentary suppositions that we might have about what our whole understanding will be. An envisionment is always either in a state of developing or available to develop further. In this sense, envisionments are "meaning-in-motion."

I call the act of knowledge development "envisionment building." Who we are, what we have experienced, what the topic is, the technologies that help us along the path of knowledge building, our relations with the environment, tools, or message—all affect the particular knowledge we build. Even when we reject and build arguments against ideas to which we are exposed, we are building envisionments of the ideas and concepts. We build envisionments all the time, in all corners of our lives, when we learn to ski, study carbon footprints, or read a book.

For example, during the 2008 presidential race, a friend gave me a book to read—*Team of Rivals* by Doris Kearns Goodwin (2005). Although I had meant to read this book about Abraham Lincoln sooner, it remained on my night table until Barack Obama was elected the 44th president of the United States. Then, because I had heard how much Obama had been influenced by Lincoln's words and deeds and how closely he had studied Lincoln, I felt I had to read the book. Even before I opened the cover, I began the act of envisionment building. What would the book be like? What portions of Lincoln's presidency would it cover? I was certain that his political life, his presidency, and the Civil War would be highlighted, but what else? I also knew that Lincoln could not have acted alone to achieve his ends and remembered that he had been good at building support, that he was an excellent politician. But how did he do this? And how accurate would the book be?

In the beginning I had some suppositions, a few ideas, and very many questions. Then I read on the cover that Doris Kearns Goodwin had been awarded the Pulitzer Prize and the Lincoln Prize for this book, so I felt that it had been fairly well vetted for accuracy. Although I hadn't yet read a page, my act of envisionment building had begun.

I began my reading, open to what I could learn. But I read with a particular purpose. I wanted to see connections between President Lincoln and President Obama. And so my quest began. As I read about Lincoln's early personal hardships and his steadfast persistence, I easily connected them to what I already knew about Obama's youth, especially from his book *Dreams from My Father* (1995), which I mentioned in the previous chapter. With this slim beginning, I began to build a fuller envisionment, making assumptions about how each had used his early experiences as an impetus to develop a strong sensitivity to human need, a strong desire to succeed, an affable personality, and a calm and thoughtful demeanor. Each crafted himself to be a well-informed, inclusive, and just leader. As I read, I looked for evidence that might reinforce this aspect of my envisionment. I remembered noting some of these qualities in Obama during his campaign, and saw more and more evidence of these qualities in Lincoln, especially from Kearns's description of the 1860 Republican Convention, where Lincoln won the nomination, and continuing throughout his presidency. As I read further, I found evidence of even more similarities between Lincoln and Obama, including their desire to lead, their political shrewdness and canniness, their ability to incorporate rivals into their administration, their pragmatism, and their ability to stand above jealousy and disagreement, as well as their willingness to take chances and take charge.

You can see that as I began the book, I had a few knowns, some maybes, and a lot of questions. But as I read on, and made comparisons on my own, I began to go beyond hunches to develop assumptions, form ideas, and read ahead for evidence that would support or challenge my ideas, always comparing them with what I had already read or heard about Obama's campaign and presidency. Throughout the reading, as additional data became available to me, my envisionments changed and grew. I was able to fill in details as some essential similarities became clearer.

When I finished the book, I read Obama's inauguration speech online to identify specific points of overlap. Since then, I've also scanned the Internet, watched TV news and political discussions, and read the news to keep up with his decisions and the ways in which he handles his problems, always leaving room for changing envisionments as my knowledge grows.

As I said in introducing this section, the word *envisionment* refers to the understanding we have at any point in time, whether it is growing during reading, being tested against new information, or kept on hold awaiting new input. Even after we have closed the book and the last images or words have faded, we are left with an envisionment that is subject to change. That envisionment contains varying questions and hunches as well as more fully formed ideas, images, disagreements, and arguments. There is always the likelihood that more information, experience, or insight will cause us to clarify, extend, or in some other way alter our understanding. All this is part of the act of envisionment building. It is our path to knowledge.

Interacting with Texts in a Mathematics Class

In classrooms, students' envisionments similarly develop over time as more primary documents are read, more experiments are carried out, more simulations are completed, or more discussions take place. Look at Oscar, a high school junior. Both he and his teachers consider him a low-average student. Math is his worst subject, and he is taking general math. To help students learn to think mathematically, their teacher, Tony Massina*, sometimes has them read recently published articles that have some math principles or computations they can discuss and, when appropriate, make further calculations. He found one such article, "A Molecular Checkup," in the February 2009 issue of *Scientific American* (Renne, 2009).

Below is part of Oscar's think-aloud as he read that article. (In my studies, I often ask students to read aloud and express their thoughts as they are reading, as a way for them to provide me with a window on their thinking. In this case, Oscar's class was reading the article to themselves as he read it aloud to me in a nearby room.) His reading of words from the text of the article is in italics. Oscar's thoughts are in brackets. The correct words for those he mispronounced are in parentheses.

Oscar is interested in science. Watch his envisionment building.

A Molecular Checkup

[Uh oh. I have no idea about what this is going to be about. I know what molecules are, but not too much.]

Not long ago cancer medicine in the U.S. passed a hopeful milestone: for the first time, the incidental (incidence) rates for both new cases and deaths in men and women declined. . . . [This sounds good. But I don't know why.] Between 1999 and 2005 diagnosis rates dropped annually, by about 0.8 percent. [Eight-tenths of 1 percent, that doesn't sound like a lot to me.] Although deaths from some specific conditions have gone up, overall the mortal from cancer [oh, mortality] is on the decline for both men and women of almost all ethnic groups [maybe Dominicans, too], as it has been since the early 1990's, in large part because of a shrinking toll from malignants (malignancies) of the lung, prostate, breast [yeah, my mother had breast cancer] and colon.

That good news invites some cautious interpretation. Incidence rates might have fallen because fewer patients are going for mammograms [I thought they were good], prostate screening tests and other diagnostic procedures; if so, physicians may not yet be aware of cases that will eventually surface. [I get it, but the numbers might still be the same, eh?] The drop in mortality statistics may largely reflect the population's healthier way of life [We're supposed to be eating better—maybe]—most significantly, its decision to kick the tobacco habit. [I think that's it, it really makes a difference.]

To keep this anti, um, cancer (anticancer) momentum, therefore, health care will surely need to step up prevention and treatment in ways that are more tolerable [I don't know that word] and affordable for the general public. [But they said that the numbers were down. Why are they saying they need to do more? Maybe they think they can get rid of it? Make it disappear?]

Oscar continues to read the next section very carefully, to learn whether his supposition that they are trying to make cancer disappear is correct and what they are thinking of. As the article continues, it describes some possibilities in nanomedicine that interest him. He tries hard to understand its possibilities.

You can see that as Oscar begins reading, he thinks he has no idea what the article is going to be about. He tries to make connections between what he is reading and his own life to start building an envisionment. He tries to make initial sense of the article. He reads on and makes connections to what he already knows about cancer, healthy living, and their interrelationships. As his reading continues, we see him getting caught up in the ideas and beginning to grapple with possibilities himself. When his own ideas come to mind in response to the text, as well as when he reads new information in the text, his envisionment becomes fuller. Oscar is learning some things about cancer and future possibilities for its prevention that he didn't know before. He still is uncertain about the numbers.

Mr. Massina will follow this reading by having the students compute 0.8 percent of the population of the United States and giving them some other statistics about cancer to unpack, check, and discuss. This, in turn, will lead the students to raise other questions and look for solutions. All of the parts—the text, the computations, and the discussions that accompany them—collectively lead Oscar to an even fuller envisionment. Similar to my own building a richer envisionment of the Lincoln–Obama connection, Oscar is in the process of creating his understanding of the article, and also going beyond it to understand the numerical scope of the problem of cancer in the United States and, later, the mathematics principles behind the computations.

Oscar's interest in this article and the ideas he thought of were a function of his life, his experiences, and his values. He wasn't too sure that people are eating more healthily, although he knows it is recommended that they do. He began as a skeptic, but got caught up by the information he was reading about and the possibilities it suggested. Like Oscar, students in all courses experience many changes in their envisionments as they explore new content through their reading, viewing, Internet searching, discussion, and writing. Their envisionments change as their thoughts are provoked. New problems provoke new suppositions that move the thinking along. Minds are in motion as meaning builds.

In this way, envisionment building is an act of sense-making, one that contributes to knowledge. There is a constant interaction between the person, his or her culture, background, and knowledge, as well as the context in which the thinking is taking place. All affect what comes to mind (e.g., Oscar's comments about his mother, his Dominican heritage, and the 0.8 percent). In this sense, an envisionment is always personal. An envisionment encompasses what an individual thinks, feels, senses, and knows, often tacitly, as understandings develop. Therefore, in any school subject, although there is a common core of understanding that will overlap from student to student, the envisionments that students build will always be their own.

STANCES DURING ENVISIONMENT BUILDING

Before we leave this introduction to envisionment building, let us consider the kinds of knowledge that learners call upon as they are in the act of making sense, whether the learner is an adult reading *Team of Rivals,* a student in Mr. Massina's class, or you. From the start, learners have a number of ways in which they can relate to the material they are learning; I call them *stances*. Stances are crucial to the act of knowledge building because each stance offers a different vantage point from which to gain ideas. The stances are not linear; they can and often do recur at various points in the learning process. There are five stances I have identified. (Although I identified four stances in Langer, 1995, I have since added a fifth stance.) In each stance, the learner is in a different position in relationship to the material being learned.

Being Out and Stepping Into an Envisionment

When we encounter new material, we try to gather enough ideas to get a sense of what it will be about. This is the place where we begin a conversation with ourselves or others in an attempt to locate clues to potentially related things that we already know. Think about Oscar's first comments while reading. Because there was little for him to build on, at the outset he was outside the envisionment. In this stance, our search is for breadth rather than depth. It involves what is colloquially called "poking around" (or snooping or sweeping for ideas); we search without knowing what we are looking for. To do this, we search surface features of the material that is presented and any other available clues. We begin to locate potentially relevant ideas and connect them to what we know, build related expectations, raise content-specific questions, and seek further ideas and evidence. It is from these searches that we step into envisionments, however thin. They contain our initial ideas and suppositions about the topic, the nature of the material, and how we might relate to it.

Being In and Moving Through an Envisionment

From these initial ideas and experiences with the topic, we become more immersed in narrowing the possibilities and developing understandings. We use the material, personal knowledge, and the disciplinary or social context to furnish ideas and spark our thinking, as I did with *Team of Rivals* and Oscar did with "A Molecular Checkup." As this occurs, we become more and more immersed in building our understandings. We elaborate on what we know, make connections, and enrich our understandings. We fill out our shifting sense of where we are going with the ideas.

Stepping Out and Rethinking What You Know

This stance is essentially different from the others. In the other stances we use our knowledge and experiences to make sense of the envisionments we are building. In this stance, we use our developing envisionments in order to learn from, better understand, or rethink our own knowledge or experiences. Although we build envisionments toward knowledge in the other stances, here we step out and become aware of what we know and question, if not revise, our prior knowledge or experience based on these new understandings.

Stepping Out and Objectifying the Experience

The fourth stance is the most analytical; it involves going deeper and reaching out. Here, we distance ourselves from our envisionments, analyze, synthesize, and judge them. This stance, then, serves as a reflection on our own envisionment building and moves us to an awareness of our knowledge development. We also make comparisons to other related knowledge, sources, and situations. We think critically, focusing on the quality of the meanings, their relevance to each other, and their relationships to other things we know about or are studying.

Leaving an Envisionment and Going Beyond

This fifth stance occurs far less often than the others. It represents the times when we have built sufficiently rich and well-developed envisionments that we have knowledge available to use in new and sometimes unrelated situations. Thus, we can move from the one learning experience to another, from one richly developed envisionment to the beginnings of a new one. To do this we select critical concepts from the present envisionment and enter into a new envisionment-building experience, making connections and drawing on our previous knowledge.

THE STANCES AS AN INSTRUCTIONAL TOOL

Above, I have described the stances as they occur in situations where people have their first experiences with materials, data, or ideas. They can, however, also be a useful framework for thinking about instruction.

In moving the five stances into the classroom, we can think of the five stances as:

1. Getting Started with the Material
2. Developing Understanding of the Material
3. Learning from the Material
4. Thinking Critically About the Material
5. Going Beyond the Material

Each stance suggests a different set of questions or activities that can support students in the process of building envisionments around new concepts and ideas within their subject-area classrooms. For example, many teachers have found it useful to prepare "Envisionment-Building Guides" using these five instructional stances when they plan their lessons. These guides consist of a set of questions they can ask during class discussion time as a way to help their students think about the material. Each question encourages students to focus on one of the five stances. Asking these questions in whole-class discussion provides both students and teachers with overt windows into the students' understanding of the material and helps teachers plan the kinds of support that their students need in order to think more clearly and deeply.

Teachers often find it useful to begin with a generic Envisionment-Building Guide, and then tailor the questions based on the particular topic they are teaching. Here, for example, is a generic Envisionment-Building Guide for social studies/history.

An Envisionment-Building Guide for Teachers: Social Studies/History

Getting Started with the Material. Here, students use their background knowledge and what they have read or been introduced to as a way to enter into an initial envisionment. They begin to make a mental picture of the material. Types of questions to tap their related knowledge follow:

- What do you think the topic of this video program/chapter/original document will be?
- What do you think we'll be learning about?
- How does it connect to what we've discussed before/what you know about this topic?
- About when do you think this happened? Under what conditions?

- How do you think this relates to what we've been studying?
- Do you have any questions? Be specific.

Developing Understanding of the Material. Here, students move through the material. They connect relevant details and build upon them to make a more cohesive envisionment. Meaning builds upon meaning and leads to a richer understanding. Types of questions to tap their developing understandings follow:

- How does this material add to or differ from what you already know about this topic?
- What seems most important to you about what we've been studying? Tell why.
- What particular way does this author (presenter) want you to think about the topic?
- What are some different perspectives we can take on this topic? Discuss and provide evidence.
- Summarize what we've just seen/read/discussed.
- How do these events relate to the social, economic, political, or geographic conditions of the time?
- What other events from the past or present does this remind you of? How do they connect?
- Based on what you already know, is there something else that could have been done?

Learning from the Material. Here, students step out of the envisionment they are building and examine any new ideas it may offer or any existing ideas it may change. They are aware that there is a change in their understanding. Types of questions to tap learning from the material follow:

- How does what we've been studying make you think differently about this person/event/era/situation?
- Did the material make you rethink anything you thought you knew about the topic?
- Is there a lesson about history or human behavior that you can take away from this? Discuss.
- What did you learn about the topic that you didn't know before?
- In what way could this material make a major change in how you think about this person, country, event, or era?

Thinking Critically About the Material. Here, students step out of the envisionments they have built and objectively examine the events, issues, data, concepts, and related social occurrences and effects. They consider causes and their effects, problems and their solutions. They also make comparisons between the construct at hand and others across time, cultures, civilizations, and individuals, and offer critiques. They evaluate sources in terms of reliability or bias. Types of questions to tap thinking critically about the material follow:

- Analyze and interpret the situation/ideas/actions in terms of the era (or country or setting) in which it took place. How might it differ if it had taken place in another time (or country or setting)? Explain.
- What aspects of the presentation show a bias? Discuss what they are and how they affect your reaction to the information.
- Analyze and critique the treatment of the topic or the information given. Provide evidence to support your critique.
- Analyze and make judgments about the situation from the perspective of the various people and places involved. Provide data and compare and contrast.
- Synthesize the major points and, with a concept map or other visual, show how they relate to one another.

Going Beyond the Material. Here, students leave their thoughts about the particular material behind and use ideas and issues that have made an impact on them to create new uses or adaptations, or consider new social issues. Types of questions to get at going beyond the material follow:

- How do the ideas we've been discussing contribute to a larger conversation about central concepts in this discipline?
- How do the ideas we have been discussing contribute to a larger conversation about discovery, history, and social change? (Think about other courses you have taken or current events in the world.)
- Discuss the issues and actions in terms of their place in history and their lesson for the future.
- What would happen if we took what we learned here and used it as a new way to think about what is happening today or in another social/historical period?

If you can determine the stances from which the students are responding, you can ask questions, such as those listed above, as ways to help them enter unused stances to enrich their interpretations and deepen their understandings.

SUMMING UP

Envisionment building is the act of making sense. It happens over time as we engage with what we know, ask questions, make connections, confront our confusions and preconceptions, refine our understandings, and move beyond our momentary thoughts about the material.

Envisionments represent our understanding and questions at a particular point in time. They are always open to new input and fresh perspectives. Envisionment building is enriched by the variety of stances that we take toward the evolving envisionment: getting started with the material, developing understanding, learning from the material, thinking critically, and going beyond. These stances offer different vectors into a common problem or goal and bring us different kinds of understandings. Together they have the potential to expand our knowledge.

But the process of envisionment building also differs depending upon what we are looking for during the knowledge-building process—whether we have a clear point of reference that we are exploring, or are instead considering ever-evolving possibilities. We will turn to the differences this intention makes in the next chapter.

NOTE

1. I was first introduced to the concept of *envisionment* when, in 1980, I worked on a federally funded reading-comprehension-test research project with Charles Fillmore and Paul Kay, who were the principal investigators. Fillmore said that he had heard John Seely Brown use the term in a discussion of active thought during debugging in mathematics. Suzanne Langer's (1942) use of "envisagements" is related. In the years since, I have continued to develop it in ways that have made it essential to my understanding of how people go about making sense, how they build knowledge, and what teachers must do to help their students gain knowledge. See Langer, 1990, 1995, 2004, and 2010 for further discussion.

CHAPTER 3

How We Build
Literate Knowledge

I have already suggested that we build knowledge by feeding our ever-changing envisionments with ideas, questions, hunches, reflections, judgments, and rethinkings. These acts help us refine our understandings by asking new and different questions and move us to acquire knowledge. Information is superficial; it is on the surface of understanding. However, knowledge is deep; connections are made in ways that open conceptual understanding and lead to long-term memory, retrievability, and usability.

Although all envisionment building involves a process of knowledge growth and knowledge building, the nature of this process is quite different based on the orientation that a person takes toward the knowledge-building experience. Let us discuss this next.

ORIENTATIONS TOWARD MEANING

When we are building envisionments, what kind of meaning do we seek and expect? My work shows that people engage in envisionment building all the time when they are making sense, but there are basic differences in ways they orient themselves toward meaning—in how people position their minds to expect ideas, based on their primary purpose for the activity (Langer, 1990).

When our goal is to get information and build concepts, we expect to come away with some knowledge related to the topic we are investigating, and we use that topic as the focus of our thinking. On the other hand, when our goal is to reconnoiter or discover, we expect to be filled with thoughts and images that we didn't imagine when we began the experience. In this case, our focus changes as our understanding grows. Both orientations are discussed in more detail in the sections that follow.

Maintaining a Point of Reference

When our purpose is primarily to gain concepts or information, our orientation involves "maintaining a point of reference." I use the word *point* because there is generally a particular kind of information we are after, at least in some broad sense. I use the word *reference* because we narrow in on what we think is related information and filter out what we think is irrelevant. We focus on increasingly more specific meaning. When we start to read an article, for example, we typically have a general idea of what it will be about—from its title, perhaps, as well as where it has been published. If not, we use the opening paragraphs to establish a better sense of the topic—what the content is about or the author's point of view. Once decided upon, this sense of the whole becomes a steady reference point that guides our reading.

As the experience progresses, we try to build upon, clarify, or modify our momentary understandings and check them to see how well they contribute to our understanding of the whole. As we move along, we seek to remove ambiguities and build a web of understandings, all related to the particular topic or set of ideas we are thinking about. But we rarely change our overall sense of what the topic, the article, the book or documentary is about—unless, of course, there is enough contradictory information to change our minds. In point-of-reference thinking, our sense of the whole changes only when we encounter a substantial amount of countervailing evidence.

Exploring Horizons of Possibilities

In contrast, a reconnaissance orientation involves an open-ended search. I call it "exploring horizons of possibilities." I use the word *exploring* because we engage in a reconnaissance activity when we don't have a firm sense of what to look for. We need to collect data and let the experience lead us to meaning. When we are in a reconnaissance experience, we ponder new ideas, calling on all we know, have experienced, and can imagine, to give us a fuller picture of the images that come to mind.

I use the words *horizons of possibilities* because, as we ponder new possibilities, the overall sense of where our understandings may go continually changes. When we read a novel or watch a film, for example, our sense of how it will end, and what it will mean, changes as events unfold and characters develop. Each new action or episode not only increases our understanding of what has come before, but opens up new horizons along with an array of possibilities for our understanding of the work as a whole.

Over time, I have broadened my description of the act of "exploring horizons of possibilities" in ways that still incorporate the literary acts I described earlier (Langer, 1990, 1995), yet more explicitly capture the open-ended "reconnaissance" activity that extends across all disciplines.

When exploring horizons of possibilities, our thinking works on two planes simultaneously. It is as if we are rubbing our stomachs and tapping our heads at the same time. We might ask (from *Saraband*, the last Ingmar Bergman film), "Why did she go back to see him after all those years? Will all the old patterns repeat themselves?" As you consider alternative answers, the ways you imagine the story may end will change. We may be exploring a relationship at the moment, but it also makes us look at the implications for the meanings we find in the film—and the future of their time together. This is the double open-endedness that comes from exploring possibilities. It isn't an empty open-endedness, but one that is filled with possibilities that are always tentative—waiting for other possibilities to come into view. Each time our acts of reconnaissance lead us to consider different data, perspectives, eras, cultures, or life situations, our sense of the whole changes; it continues to develop as the envisionment unfolds.

HOW THE ORIENTATIONS AFFECT INSTRUCTION

Let me contrast horizons of possibilities and point-of-reference thinking further with an example from the investigations of baseball players who were accused of taking drugs to enhance their performance, and the baseball commission's overall effort to clean up the sport. If I were orchestrating a discussion in a classroom, I could ask:

1. What is the main purpose of major league baseball?
2. What are the main goals of the players? Of their coaches?
3. What do you know about the problems with baseball players or other athletes taking drugs?
4. Why are these drugs banned?
5. What steps to stop drug-taking have various sports commissions undertaken to "clean up" their sport?

6. Major League Baseball has been doing random drug tests for a few years. Based on the various scandals, have the tests been effective?
7. Based on what we've discussed, what do you think needs to be done now?

Or I could ask:

1. What did you think when you heard A-Rod's confession that he had taken steroids some years before they were made illegal? What was your reaction?
2. Did it make you think of Michael Phelps, the Olympic gold-medal swimmer, who admitted using marijuana even though he knew it was illegal? Let's talk about it.
3. Did you think either of them should have been punished? Explain.
4. Have you read about the doping problem in sports? Have you talked about it with other people? Discuss.
5. What is your reaction to random drug tests? What about the athletes' reactions? Their sponsors? Why?
6. Based on what we've discussed, what do you think needs to be done now?

Which set of questions are more likely to provoke point-of-reference thinking and which are more likely to promote horizons-of-possibilities thinking, the first or the second? Both sets of questions could be useful; they simply invite different kinds of thinking. The first set invites us to remember what we have learned from newspapers, TV news, and other sources. The focus is on clarity and fullness of the information. It invites point-of-reference thinking. On the other hand, the second set starts closer to our own experience and helps us think about it. It invites a broader and more open-ended search for ideas we can connect with, including personal interactions, gossip, newspapers, and blogs, each bringing reactions, agreements, disagreements, points of view, and perhaps yet other questions. This set invites the exploration of horizons of possibilities. Look back to see that the final question is the same in both sets. However, it is likely to be answered somewhat differently as a result of the orientation established by the questions leading up to it.

The goal of point-of-reference thinking is to understand something more fully when:

1. We know what the topic or the information we're after is, but know little about it—we want to access that information and to think about it.
2. We know something about the topic, but want to understand it more fully—to refine and expand our understandings about it.
3. We want to use the content generatively, as a stepping-stone to creating new uses or applications for our knowledge.

The goal of exploring horizons of possibilities is to create a new conceptualization when:

1. There is something new we want to think about or develop.
2. There is a problem we're having difficulty solving.
3. We are not sure where we are headed.

In both orientations we maintain a sense of the whole, but the nature of those wholes is different. Our point-of-reference thinking is constrained by our sense of the topic, while exploring horizons of possibilities is constrained by our ability to imagine possibilities. In one case, we think within the constraints of the particular information we seek, while in the other case the questions and the possibilities we can explore are open-ended, giving us room to find new horizons.

HOW THE ORIENTATIONS RELATE TO ONE ANOTHER

I have suggested that when we build envisionments, we can maintain a point of reference or we can explore horizons of possibilities. Each of these requires us to orient ourselves differently toward the meanings we will build. Of course, we can move from one to another (and often do), but at any point in time, one is usually more primary. The question then is: How do maintaining a point of reference and exploring horizons of possibilities relate to one another? Can they be used in ways that help students gain deeper and more lasting knowledge in the disciplines as well as prepare them to use their knowledge most fruitfully in their years ahead?

There is evidence that the processes involved in these approaches to thinking are important and productive in dealing with problems of everyday life and work. For example, a study of physicians (Elstein, Shulman, & Sprafka, 1978) found that throughout their professional training they learn to match the symptoms to a cause and make a diagnosis by using point-of-reference thinking. But when this method of thinking is unproductive, they create more fluid scenarios that come to mind based on a variety of situations they have experienced or know about. They are on a reconnaissance mission to find possible clues that they can apply to their problem. Here, they keep the endpoint (in this case, the diagnosis) open while exploring many possibilities from many perspectives, and seeing where they might lead.

From 1997–2007, the *New Yorker* published a series of articles by a physician, Jerome Groopman (2007), describing a variety of hard-to-solve medical cases. Each article was about a patient with a medical problem that resisted diagnosis and treatment. In each case the physicians ran many tests, all the ones they could think of that were at all appropriate for the symptoms the patients displayed. Yet, after guarded diagnoses and treatment, the patients did not get better. The doctors tested again and prescribed again. But, in each case, the doctors were stumped; they attempted to make well-founded diagnoses, but none held up. When they finally arrived at a treatment that worked, it was because they moved away from their usual diagnostic procedures and engaged in the more fluid and open-ended form of thinking that we are calling exploring horizons of possibilities. And then, with a new diagnosis, they returned to point-of-reference thinking to prescribe a new treatment. They drew on the strengths of both orientations, with good results.

Similar studies have been done with lawyers preparing difficult court cases (Dworkin, 1983) and with people who repair highly complex computers (Orr, 1987). In each case, when the situation is complicated and the end point unclear, the two orientations are used together to find new solutions and then put them into place. The ability to use point of reference and the ability to use horizons of possibilities are natural and necessary parts of the well-developed intellect, complementing one another.

Other commentators have discussed similar processes at work in the field of science. Arthur Koestler (1964) talks about people needing to make "shifts of attention" to experiences that previously had been seen as irrelevant, helping them see things in a new, revealing light. He sees the shift from one mode of thought to the other as being productive, as potentially bringing in more information. He also suggests that all creative activities have a pattern in common, that artists' creative activities have similar psychological qualities to those of scientists. In both cases, there is a continuous move from objective to subjective—from verifiable proof to subjective experience. The facts or data are needed but are not enough; Koestler suggests that the successive patterns in which data are arranged and rearranged are at the heart of new ideas. We can view these shifts as moving between maintaining a point of reference (in which data are arranged) and exploring horizons of possibilities (in which attention shifts).

Koestler's ideas are quite resonant with our discussion so far. They not only acknowledge both orientations to meaning-making as being important, but also emphasize that exploring horizons of possibilities is a highly desirable activity in all fields, working together with point-of-reference thinking.

The Example of Gutenberg

As an example of how they work together in very useful ways, let me tell you about Johannes Gutenberg and the invention of the printing press. Koestler uses this case as an example of creativity in science, and I use it here to illustrate ways in which point of reference and exploring horizons of possibilities work together in knowledge growth. As I describe Gutenberg's experiences, watch how his envisionments of what will become his printing press change over time.

By the beginning of the 15th century, printing already had a long history (it started as early as the 12th century). To print on paper, wooden blocks were engraved in relief with pictures, text, or both. They were then wet with ink and a sheet of paper was laid on the block and rubbed until the impression was transferred from the block to the paper. Each sheet could only be printed on one side, with the blank sides pasted together and bound into "block books." Gutenberg wanted to print the Bible for mass use. In a letter to a friend, he wrote (all indented quotes are from Koestler, 1964, pages 121–124):

> For a month my head has been working. . . . You have seen, as I have, playing cards and pictures of saints [made by the block printing method]. . . .
> Well, what has been done for a few words, for a few lines, I must succeed in doing for large pages of writing, for large leaves covered on both sides, for whole books, for first of all, the bible. . . . How?

> It is useless to think of engraving on pages of wood the whole thirteen hundred pages. . . . What am I to do? I do not know: but I know what I want to do. I wish to manifold the bible. . . .

Gutenberg knew what he wanted his invention to do, but had no notion of what it would look like or how it would do it. He begins with horizons of possibilities thinking, on a reconnaissance mission. After an initial search, he turned to coin-printing. He noticed that

> Every coin begins with a punch. The punch is a little rod of steel with the shape of one letter. . . . The punch is moistened and driven into steel which becomes the "hollow. . . ."

Here, he is examining this process using point-of-reference thinking. He goes on to explain that these hollows are moistened, and gold is placed inside them, then the punch is used to turn the gold into coins with powerful blows. So, now we see Gutenberg beginning to explore an early notion of what would become the art of typecasting. But he wanted a clearer print, so he kept exploring possibilities. Some time later, he wrote,

> I took part in the wine harvest. I watched the wine flowing, and going back from effect to cause, I studied the [wine] press which nothing can resist. . . .

Here, he made a connection between the possibilities of the wine press action and the "horizons" of his printer that had been shifting in his mind over time. It occurred to him that steady pressure of feet pressing the grapes on paper would leave a trace on the paper.

> One must strike, cast . . . letters in relief . . . and the punch for producing them like your foot when it multiplies a print. There is the Bible!

So, Gutenberg put together in new ways a number of the reference points he had come to understand with some possibilities he had explored, and these led to a new whole—the first printing press. He started with an idea of what he wanted to accomplish, but to do this it was necessary for him not only to maintain certain points of reference but also to explore horizons of possibilities until one horizon gave him the basis for his printing press.

FOSTERING BOTH ORIENTATIONS IN DISCIPLINARY CLASSES

Some educators believe that science involves only tight logical thinking and that to move away from it is to "muddy" or "loosen" the thinking. But the examples we have seen, from doctors, lawyers, computer repair, and Gutenberg, suggest that this isn't at all the case. The logic of point-of-reference thinking is important, but so, too, is the power of new ideas that comes from exploring horizons of possibilities. So, there is a schism. On the one hand, in many fields of education, objectivity, logic, and deductive reasoning are considered "good thinking," and when students move away from this and begin to explore possibilities (especially from outside the field of data), they are stopped and are considered errant, doing sloppy work. On the other hand, we see from examples in life that even in disciplines that largely deal with abstract symbols, there is an interrelationship between the objective and the subjective—with the two together allowing for deeper, fuller, and sometimes new and exciting understandings in all subjects (Csikszentmihalyi, 1996; Gardner, 2008; Koestler, 1964; Kuhn, 1962; Sternberg, Grigorenko, & Singer 2004).

From this perspective, the more limited view of thinking must be broadened, to permit students to learn to engage productively in both orientations. Teachers in the various subject areas need to incorporate both orientations into the ways they help students develop their understanding of course material. Their questions, assignments, and instructional materials must engage students in exploring horizons of possibilities as well as maintaining a point of reference, if students are to develop the knowledge they need to make new discoveries as well as to understand previous solutions.

A Social Studies/History Class Studying Ancient Egypt

Let me give you a brief example of how students' envisionments of King Tut and his reign change and become enriched as they move back and forth between maintaining points of reference and exploring horizons of possibilities. This is Cara Monteiro's* 6th-grade social studies/history class (11-year-olds) with students from a wide range of abilities and backgrounds. They were studying ancient Egypt. To begin, they saw a play about King Tut and, through discussion, explored horizons of possibilities to gain some initial understanding of the circumstances surrounding Tut and his reign. Then they searched the Internet for information about ancient Egyptian culture, and read the part of their textbook on the pha-raohs. Here, point of reference was the dominant approach to meaning-making. Then they read other books for additional information. This involved point-of-reference reading as well.

During each activity, as the students read the materials before them, they made reader's marks (text annotations) in the margins of their reading material, to identify parts they didn't understand (?), connections they were making (C), parts that they didn't expect or surprised them (S), and so forth. Next, they filled in an "open mind" diagram (an outline of an "empty" head that needed to be filled in) with all they had learned about leadership in ancient Egypt from the multiple sources as well as the play, and discussed their understandings. Then they took part in a "Stand and Deliver" activity in which the teacher gave four examples of what King Tut might have done in a particular situation. The students individually decided which of the four actions was most likely and defended their point of view with evidence, moving between the two orientations as they considered possibilities and then sought evidence to support them. (All three of these activities are described in Adler & Rougle, 2005).

At this point, Ms. Monteiro felt her students were on the road to deeper understanding of the problems of leadership in Tut's era, but she wanted to push their ideas further. To do this, she developed a discussion guide with open-ended questions meant to move students to and through various kinds of deeper comprehension. The questions required the students to return to their texts to answer the questions in order to clarify their ideas, and then they had to discuss them with one another. They had to agree, disagree with, add to, or challenge one another's views, explain and defend their own—and tell why, with evidence. Point-of-reference thinking was used as students explained and defended their ideas, but sometimes they stepped back and explored new possibilities, particularly when they were uncertain or when their ideas were challenged.

This turned into a highly substantive discussion of whether King Tut had played a part in his own death. The students discussed problems of leadership in an era of religious and political turmoil, analyzed the essence of heroism, and related these problems to other leaders they had studied. They also discussed similarities with today's world, and suggested lessons from the past that could inform the decisions of today.

For a class of 11-year-olds with a wide range of academic ability, there was a great deal of thoughtful involvement. The students came away with especially deep understandings not only of the reign of King Tut, but also of leadership—in a worldwide, national, and everyday sense as well.

The two kinds of thinking that Ms. Monteiro invited permitted this rich learning to happen. The orientations the students took varied based on the particular question, their understanding of the topic, and their perceived goal. The questions and guidance that Ms. Monteiro offered, based on her perceptions of how best to advance her students' thinking about the content, permitted them to gain substantial understandings of the essential issues they were studying.

SUMMING UP

The distinctions between exploring horizons of possibilities and maintaining a point of reference can help teachers understand how they can support students to think well and gain knowledge in all subjects. The kinds of questions teachers ask, the kinds of assignments they give, and the kinds of tests they fashion—what is considered evidence of doing well—change based on the primary purpose of the activity as well as the discipline. From an envisionment-building perspective, teachers try to help students develop different reasoning strategies and also come to qualitatively different understandings when the reading, discussion, and other activities are for horizons of possibilities as opposed to point of reference purposes. The ability to use both will hold students in good stead for the rest of their lives. The question you may be asking is, "How do you make an envisionment-building classroom work?" We will turn to that in the next chapter.

CHAPTER 4

Envisionment-Building Classrooms

Let me begin this chapter by telling you about a French class I am taking. The course is titled *"Conversation et Grammaire."* It is considered a review class and meets for 2 hours once a week. My professor, Madame Lescaut*, is an experienced teacher whom I had never met before the course began. The first day, after asking each of us to introduce ourselves, she told us she wanted help in deciding which text to use. She said that the one she liked best cost $70 and passed around a few copies for us to look at as she explained (in French),

> What I particularly like about this book is that each section begins with an interesting story or article. Then, all the grammar and vocabulary exercises are based wholly on the readings. We can discuss what we read, see how the grammar works, and then do some exercises that are based on both the piece and the grammar. It's all woven together. Let's look at the first piece to see what I mean. . . .

Of course, we voted to spend the $70.

Then she said, "Now let's get ready for your first reading assignment." She spent the next 15 minutes telling us what the story, *"Le Symbole"* by Bernard Dadie (2001), was about, then lectured us on tense forms, listing the tenses on the SMART Board and giving us examples of how they are used—never mentioning or referring back to the story. Toward the end of the 2-hour class, she gave us *les devoirs,* our homework assignment. She did not try to learn what we already knew about the author or the topic of the piece (African-French immigrants in French schools), nor did she engage us in thinking about any of these in advance of reading. She never tried to learn the extent of our knowledge of the tense forms she so assiduously lectured about. Nor, except for our 2-minute self-introduction, did we students ever have a chance to speak.

I thought the second class would be better because we had purchased the text and read the next story in advance. Guess what? We spent the first 40 minutes taking turns reading the grammar exercises we had done for homework (rewriting sentences about the story in a particular called-for tense). Each student recited two sentences; this continued round-robin until each of the exercises was done. If we were right, she said so, and if we were wrong, she corrected us and, at times, lectured us about the usage. Madame never invited the rest of the class to discuss either the error or what the correction might be. Nor did she ask for questions. She followed this homework review with a 1-hour review of the grammar for the following week's assignments, using the same lecture and SMART Board approach as the week before. Twenty minutes before the end of class, she said, "Now, let's turn to the story." I had prepared what I thought was an interesting insight into the characters and their situation and raised my hand to begin the discussion, but she didn't look up. She looked at her book and said, "Who can tell us what happened first?" We spent the rest of the time searching each paragraph or text section to locate the particular parts she had in mind. There was recitation, but no conversation. Our responses were in phrases, not even full sentences. She was checking our recollection of and ability to locate specific parts of the story, but not inviting a discussion of the story. She did not provide us with an opportunity to practice using the language in conversation.

The next week, at the beginning of class, I spoke up, saying, "Madame, it is so important that we have conversations in this class, can't we please have a chance to read and discuss the story first?" She looked surprised, but said, "Oh yes, this is very important," and then had us take turns reading the assigned article aloud, round-robin. Then we went on to review our grammar homework, and then on to the new grammar as we had done before. As I write this section of the book, the semester is more than two-thirds over and the format has not changed. Madame has not ever focused on our ability to develop envisionments, either of the pieces we read or of how the language works. Instead, she has structured each class to focus on things we should know, without ever trying to determine what we already know or how complete or incomplete that knowledge is. Neither has she tried to help us make connections across class meetings concerning the grammar she is teaching, the language features used, or the content. Each class meeting is a lesson unto itself.

Clearly, Madame Lescaut has some idea that conversation and participation are important, but she doesn't understand what it means to engage students in activities that involve literate thinking and envision-ment building as routes to knowledge of how the language works.

WHAT ENVISIONMENT-BUILDING CLASSROOMS LOOK LIKE

Envisionment-building classrooms are places that function as communi-ties of inquiry. Students are engaged with working out problems, while using the processes, symbols, language, and ways of thinking that are ap-propriate to the discipline. In a sense, they are learning the culture of the discipline. They are encouraged to use what they know and to venture into making sense of new ideas and concepts. They are in "minds-on" classes where activities and assignments are planned to invite students to become engaged with the material, to think about it, and to build upon it. Because student questions, ideas, and problem-solving are center stage, teachers have an ongoing window into what their students understand, how they go about thinking in the discipline, as well as the disciplinary vocabulary they have acquired. Such classes are quite the opposite of Mme Lescaut's classes, where students are talked *to* rather than *with*, and where the teach-er holds on to the keys of knowledge rather than sharing them with her students. In envisionment-building classrooms, students are actively en-gaged in minds-on activities that are anchored in course-appropriate and discipline-appropriate ideas and issues. Whatever the topic and whatever the medium in which they are working, students have many opportuni-ties to work with others in investigating the issues, connecting them to related knowledge, taking closer looks at how things work, and deepen-ing their understanding.

Using Critical-Thinking Strategies

In order to solve the problems they are assigned, students in envision-ment-building classrooms use the following strategies at various points in time:

- Conceptualizing the content/problem/goal they're after
- Judging the appropriateness of information
- Analyzing the data first to make sense of them and then to understand them more deeply

- Comparing the new data to what students already know, have experienced, or are just studying
- Synthesizing/connecting the data to make them cohere as a unit
- Evaluating the meaning and usefulness of data in regard to understanding the topic
- Applying the information and using it in a variety of situations
- Explaining/justifying the data, findings, interpretations, or positions
- Providing evidence that is data-based and credible
- Extending/generating new ideas, applications, and knowledge in similar and/or new settings
- Theorizing about constructs and/or their contribution to another universe of meaning

These moves are actually critical-thinking strategies that everyone should have available to use when solving problems, learning, and gaining knowledge. They are central to the act of envisionment building. In a very real sense, they are the strategies that we all use when coming to understand, and they are always contextualized within the situations in which they occur. The particular ways in which a strategy is used differ based on what the strategy is used for.

Thinking Within a Discipline

In academic learning, general critical-thinking strategies are not enough. People need to learn how to use these strategies as they work within particular contexts of use. At school, the particular contexts are the subject-area disciplines. That the content differs from discipline to discipline is obvious, but that the ways of knowing and doing (of organizing and presenting ideas) also differ is less obvious and of critical importance. The ability to construe and critique content in appropriate ways is at the heart of understanding within a discipline.

In more effective disciplinary classes (Langer, 2004), students are taught how to use these critical-thinking strategies as they dig deeper and deeper into issues, make connections, generate new ideas, and help their knowledge grow, as they engage in activities that are appropriate to the discipline. In less effective classes, on the other hand, the focus is on learning important information, but not within the context of disciplinary activity. Students are not engaged in thinking about important and fascinating issues, ideas, problems, and information within the field, and thus, they have little opportunity to learn to think and act—and eventually know—in disciplinary ways. In still other programs, critical thinking is left for reading teachers to teach, although they are generally not sufficiently knowledgeable about the various disciplines to teach more than general strategies, not the subject-specific applications that make the strategies useful in envisionment building.

FEATURES OF MINDS-ON TEACHING

There are four features of instruction that need to be present in order to ensure the kind of minds-on teaching I have been discussing (Applebee, Langer, Nystrand, & Gamoran, 2003).

1. Building Envisionments

Teachers who want their students to build rich envisionments focus not only on the content to be taught, but also on how their students think about the material and what they understand. These are the roots to teaching knowledge building. Such teachers help their students use the content they are studying to explore new knowledge, and to reflect on their misconceptions as well as on interesting or related concepts as a way to develop deeper and potentially more useful understandings. In planning instruction, the teachers are constantly reflecting on progress and making decisions about what to review and what new content, skills, or strategies to teach based on students' evolving needs. When instruction is based around activities that make students think—and that give them a stake in their ideas—all students, including those who are low performers, get deeply involved in the content and what it means. They learn the vocabulary, routines, and rules of the discipline as part and parcel of reading, writing, talking, and thinking about content. They spend their class time developing understandings as well as generating and building related and new ideas. They examine discipline-appropriate issues and topics from a variety of perspectives to problematize and clarify ideas. They learn to analyze, explain, and challenge ideas and to go beyond the given. To do this, they must also learn to provide and weigh evidence, and to question it. They also learn to connect their ideas to issues beyond the lesson in generative ways, such as organizing or reorganizing relationships among different components or selecting components from one concept or system and integrating them into a conceptual whole of another system.

An English and Social Studies/History Team. For a good example of how envisionment-building classrooms work, we can look at a series of activities on the First Amendment in the classroom of Arthea Brooks*, a middle school English teacher at Garrison School, and her social studies/history team member John Rosales*. They wanted their students to write persuasive essays, and also to understand the implications of the First Amendment for individuals' lives. They planned their envisionment-building activities to engage students in a variety of critical thinking strategies in the context of both point-of-reference and horizons-of-possibilities thinking.

The activities began with a reading of the First Amendment, followed by whole-class discussion. Beginning in a point-of-reference orientation, students had time to ask questions, comment on parts of the text, and narrow in on some initial understanding of its meaning. Then they did a "quick write" about what the First Amendment means, what it protects, and what it might mean for their lives. Here, some students continued with a point-of-reference orientation, and others shifted to horizons of possibilities, based on the way they interpreted the task as well as the extent of their knowledge. With students who didn't get started at all, Ms. Brooks and Mr. Rosales asked questions to invite them into the envisionment-building process: "What does freedom of speech allow people to do without fear? Are there any ways in which religious freedom might affect your parents or neighbors? What might it be like if you didn't have it?"

After discussing their quick writes, the students read a magazine article about the First Amendment that gave a few examples of ways in which community and individual rights had been protected. Students then worked in groups to brainstorm other examples of First Amendment protections they had heard about, read about, or could imagine. Mr. Rosales and Ms. Brooks followed this with a discussion of what it would be like without these protections, including examples from other countries. The students then made a T-chart, with examples from daily life, of behaviors and beliefs that exist because of the First Amendment and those that might occur without the First Amendment. This primarily called for a point-of-reference orientation, but left room for exploring unexpected possibilities. After more discussion, students had an opportunity to plan and then give a persuasive speech, following guidelines provided by their teachers, about the benefits of First Amendment rights, from their own perspectives. This activity offered practice in content literacy (reading, writing, discussing social studies/history content in discipline-appropriate ways).

The teachers later brought up the subject of curfews, an issue the class had discussed earlier. They asked the students how they felt about having a 10:00 P.M. curfew in their community, and then had students role-play reactions from the differing perspectives of community members: police officers, elders, parents, and businesses. The discussion primarily involved horizons-of-possibilities thinking as the students struggled to step into the shoes of their elders and imagine where each possibility might take their thinking about First Amendment rights.

The final activity was to write a persuasive paper. To help the students with this task, the teachers asked them to think about (1) their point of view, (2) how it could be supported under First Amendments rights, and (3) particular people in their community and what they would need to say to convince those people of their point of view. This last activity called for point-of-reference thinking, supported by specific evidence.

Overall, Ms. Rosales and Mr. Brooks gave their students many opportunities to use a variety of critical-thinking strategies and orientations toward meanings as a way to come to understand the particular benefits of First Amendment rights, an important part of social studies/history. In turn, these new understandings were utilized in the context of learning to write to persuade others who may have differing points of view, an important part of the English curriculum. With guidance from their teachers, the students deepened their understandings and learned to make them their own.

2. Forging Curricular Connections

A second feature of minds-on classrooms is a focus on "big conversations and connected concepts" within each discipline, and on making these connections overt to students. This feature reminds us that when we learn something well, we have a sense of what the concept or ideas mean in relation to larger issues. To support this kind of learning, students need to see links between the topic being taught and larger issues—to see how the parts connect to a larger whole.

Too often, teachers have made those links, but forget to share them with their students. For example, labeling the parts of the digestive system and learning their functions becomes an exercise in recall, whereas linking the digestive system to diet, health, or the interconnectivity of body functions opens a fuller world of meaning and makes the parts of the digestive system and its functions more fully understood—and more likely to be remembered.

Instead of simply covering the curriculum, students need to become involved in seeing how what they are studying links with what they have already studied and what they will study in the future, as well as in making connections to their daily lives, concerns in the field, or events in the world. Together, teachers and students need to make conceptual connections within and across lessons, units, courses, and grade levels. This continuity and connectedness are the glue that allows students to build knowledge in the discipline. In minds-on classrooms, students learn to see relationships among content, skills, and the purpose of the activity or assignment and how these affect the appropriate orientation to meaning, critical-thinking strategies, ways to organize ideas, selection of words, and overall presentation of ideas. These kinds of curricular connections help students learn to go beyond the key ideas to the connections that underlie disciplinary knowledge.

Middle School Social Studies/History. Here is an example from a school-in-change. Before the Partnership for Literacy had begun at Branchtree Middle School, the social studies/history teachers had ordered a new textbook about the founding of the colonies and the beginning of our country. The book seemed to have engaging narrative and inviting illustrations, but there was little meat in each chapter. After reading, there was little for students to discuss. The textbook made no overt connections from one chapter to the other, and lacked a discernible theme cutting across chapters to hold the book together. When Eija Rougle, the instructional facilitator, arrived, the students were reading each chapter as if it were a story unto itself. Although questions were being asked and answered, there was little envisionment building taking place.

Our initial work with the teachers involved helping them reconstrue the book itself as not only about the founding of the colonies, but also about diverse groups of human beings coming together and moving apart in times of change. This broad theme of "together and apart in times of change" led them to realize that they could connect the chapters in exciting ways. It also enabled them to think about a variety of research projects, additional readings, videos, and other activities that they could use to help their students probe colonial history more deeply, to compare it with some events today, and to engage both point-of-reference and horizons-of-possibilities thinking as ways to open up and focus on issues along the way. When they finished the unit, they asked their students to create an imaginary society in the future, tracing it across a number of years with the focus on their experiences in thinking about the concept of "together and apart in times of change," drawing from the unit for ideas.

During these activities, the teachers helped students identify the critical content from various sources, introduced related vocabulary they might need, and provided ways to organize their information—all this with the big idea of "together and apart in times of change" as the central "point-of-reference" focus. To make the curricular connections, the students explored "horizons of possibilities," as well as explained "points of reference" both orally and in writing. Within a fairly short time, the students changed from obedient but disinterested students to engaged and involved participants, developing connections from past to present, and defending opinions of their own in ways that made them part of the middle school social studies/history community.

3. Orchestrating Substantive and Sustained Discussion and Writing

Substantive and sustained discussion is an excellent environment in which to foster envisionment building. Nystrand (1997) has reported that discussions in the secondary school disciplinary classrooms he studied were neither substantive nor sustained. Instead, they generally lasted for no more than 15 seconds and most often involved a series of turns, with one student's comments at best peripherally connected to what others have said. On the other hand, when there is substantive and sustained discussion, students listen to and interact with one another; they are thoughtful about the topic at hand as they agree, disagree, build on others' comments, refer back to texts, and bring in other sources. Such discussion can occur when people communicate with one another face-to-face, as well as through electronic interfaces such as discussion boards or wikis. Students listen to, respond to, and push one another's thinking along as they explore horizons of possibilities and maintain points of reference. Their goal in the interaction is to delve more deeply into an idea or assumption by reflecting, inspecting, critiquing, analyzing, explaining, or defending it as a way to gain clearer understandings from the interaction. Students are truly engaged in collaborative cognition as they interact around ideas and help their own and others' ideas to grow.

The teacher plays an active role in such discussions, helping students explore the topics and understand why their ideas are substantively interesting and important, as well as pointing out problems that need to be examined. The teacher also helps students focus on critical issues by offering new and less obvious ways to think about the topic.

A High School Physics Class. Take Ken Jones* and his high school physics class as an example (Langer, 1992b). During a unit on refraction, the
students were working in groups, engaged in measuring angles of refraction. The following discussion between Mr. Jones and three students is the
result of a student's procedural question.

> *Sam*: How are we getting tenths if the light beam is like one unit
> thick?
> *Mr. Jones*: That's a good question. How are you estimating?
> *Charles*: Looking at the middle of the light beam.
> *Mr. Jones* (to Sam): You don't like that?
> *Sam*: No, it's fine.
> *Skat*: Wouldn't it be easier to do it by the edge, because the middle
> is easier to make a mistake?
> *Charles*: The edge isn't really. The middle is definitely better.
> *Mr. Jones*: Why would you say it's better to use the middle?
> *Charles*: Well, like, you have a clock with a hand. The edge is on 12,
> but it's not straight up and down. At 12, it would be straight up
> and down and you would use the middle.
> *Mr. Jones*: So, if it's a pointer of some sort, you'd use the middle of
> a pointer. But Skat is saying if you're inconsistent about using
> one edge . . .
> *Skat*: Well, see, the thing is, in *this* pointer, it would be a wedge
> of the light beam, because it can't be a pointer if it keeps on
> going. It stops and you see the very end of the point. It goes
> right up to the edge of the scale. The point is the edge of the
> light.
> *Charles*: I think it doesn't make that much difference.
> *Skat*: Neither does 7.5. ("Oohs" from students in response to Skat
> getting critical of Charles)
> *Mr. Jones*: Folks, let me tell you, I am impressed by this concern
> for accuracy. That's one of the things that comes late for high
> school students, typically. . . . Often there's little concern for
> accuracy when that can often be the difference between getting
> a good or bad lab. But you can also take accuracy too far. If we
> were arguing about one hundredth of a degree, that would
> be too far. I'm not sure it's silly to be arguing over a tenth of a
> degree. And I think you're making excellent points.

As you see, the students listened to one another and engaged in extended back-and-forth conversation as they built on what they previously had said, disagreed with others, or added new explanations for the points they made. Mr. Jones entered the conversation when he thought it would be useful to move students' thinking along, or to remind them of what Skat had said. He could have easily supplied the answer to Sam's initial question. Instead, he allowed his students to use discussion to make their own observations about the measuring procedure and to think the problem of accuracy of measurement through, as it applies to this case. In doing this, he invited his students to think like physicists, and he demonstrated the value of their discussion by complimenting them on their thinking.

4. Offering Enabling Strategies

There are two categories of teaching strategies that are most useful in helping students envision knowledge: "ways to do" and "ways to think."

In supporting "ways to do," teachers might segment new or difficult tasks and provide guidance in how to do each part, showing how it builds toward task completion. At other times, they might help students learn a sequence to follow by helping them understand what each step involves, and also ways to judge whether a task has been done well. As a result, students learn to reflect on their own actions, and their effectiveness.

For example, in an earth science class, before a research project on volcanoes, George Zank* involved his students in making a list of everything they needed to do to complete the project, but they also made a list of ways to self-check what they gathered, what they comprehended so far, and what else they needed to know. As they developed their product (in this case, a video presentation, a PowerPoint show, or a report), they were expected to revisit their list and reflect on whether their in-draft product conveyed what they had learned, and its effectiveness in doing so. At the end of the project, they used these guides to grade themselves on how well they used the strategies as well as on their final product.

"Ways to think" strategies are somewhat different. Too often, students have no idea where to look or what ideas to focus on in order to answer the teachers' questions or complete their assignments. Here, helpful teachers offer thinking scaffolds. One such scaffold is a "Think About." Students follow a thinking guide that asks open-ended questions and then points them toward the content they'll need, and how to think about it.

For example, Randall Roeser* gave his mathematics students a "Think About" when they were working on supplementary angles. He said, "I am thinking of an angle. It is a supplementary angle. What would you need to know in order to determine the degree of each angle? Think about: You only need to know one angle to get both. Why?" He had them discuss this before working in groups to determine degrees.

When Meg Cory's* English class was reading an Amy Tan short story, she asked,

> How did the narrator's feelings about being a prodigy change
> during the story? Think about:
>
> 1.   Her daydreams at the beginning of the story
> 2.   Her responses to her mother's expectations
> 3.   Her own opinion of herself
>
> Make notes for yourself and then discuss your thoughts.

George Zank offered another type of "ways to think" scaffold. In his unit on volcanoes, he asked his students to list the kinds of critical thinking that his assignment required (e.g., conceptualizing, connecting/synthesizing, comparing, analyzing, explaining, providing evidence, elaborating, extending/generating). The class discussed the students' responses, exploring what each strategy entailed and how they might go about applying it—with what possible material. They took notes and used their list as well as their notes to check their own work later.

Teachers who provide help in "Learning to Do" and "Learning to Think" know to keep watching for when they can remove that help and let students use the strategies on their own. These decisions become part of class discussion and student self-monitoring of their disciplinary growth.

In successful disciplinary classrooms, envisionment-building instruction happens as a matter of course. A variety of tools that bring meaning and stimulate thinking (e.g., reading, writing, media, graphics, and talk) are used to refine new ideas, connect them with old ones, and help students build beyond. Class becomes a time when students attempt, explore, analyze, reflect, apply, critique, and communicate about their ideas at hand. In doing so, they gain knowledge of ways to control as well as understand the ideas and images within the field, the written and spoken language through which the field expresses its meaning, and the expected patterns of disciplinary language and thought.

THE INDIVIDUAL WITHIN THE GROUP

Although instructional planning usually focuses on activities to engage a class full of students, it is important to remember that the individual students within the class will each carry different experiences with the content, with literacy, and with academic learning in general. Even with these differences, teachers can plan activities that provide room for all students to be minds-on and to gain more knowledge. For this to happen, the activity must be broad enough for all students to work at the edge of their own knowledge. The class dynamic needs to be interactive enough, within and across students and groups of students as well as students and teacher, to permit individuals to be helped and challenged to venture beyond where they are, through thought-provoking questions, hints, models, telling, showing, and research—each when appropriate. The goal, whoever the students might be, is to assist them to gain new understandings and skills, to apply them to a discipline-appropriate activity, and to eventually own them. We have seen this in the examples above; in each case, the teachers created an interactive environment where such help and learning-within-the-group occurred in the normal course of events.

Overall, in envisionment-building classrooms, students' minds are on the content at hand, and teachers' minds are on what and how the students are thinking about the material. Such teachers help students approach new content by having them explore it—hands- and minds-on, with lots of problem-solving, research, and discussion in a range of small- and large-group activities. These enable students to make sense of the ideas, explore connections, think more deeply, reflect on what they know, and go beyond. Such classes are highly engaging as well as instructive.

Further, in minds-on classes, teachers use the tools of tomorrow as well as the tools of today, in the ways they are used in society—as tools for learning as well as tools for communicating. Students are encouraged to explore ideas and become engaged in the content while using the range of tools and technologies available to them to stimulate their thinking and deepen their knowledge.

SUMMING UP

In an envisionment-building classroom, the teacher orchestrates the class as well as helps and teaches. In addition to offering needed information and explanations and serving as a disciplinary model, he or she guides the students as to where to find the information or evidence they need, and helps them learn ways to inspect it, question it, and refine it. Students learn ways to think as well as ways to do. They are minds-on, engaged in thinking through their new topic, trying to understand how it fits with what they already know, the new sense it makes as well as what to do with it in relation to class activities. Unlike Madame Lescaut's class, the discussion is truly dialogic. Students interact with one another as well as with the teacher—sharing ideas, questioning, agreeing or disagreeing, or adding to one another's ideas. Students pick up on what others have said and use it as a way to try out and shape their own ideas. They learn to tell why and to inspect what others have said. They learn to become both analytic and critical. Understandings build. *Aha*'s are heard. Students are becoming members of the disciplinary community.

We have already seen that the strategies used for envisionment building look very different in science, say, than in social studies/history. Let us look closer at how all the features I have discussed in these first four chapters come together in particular disciplinary classrooms. Each of the next four chapters will be devoted to one core discipline: social studies/history, science, mathematics, and English. Each will focus on ways that envisionment building forms the basis for rich instruction and learning.

CHAPTER 5

Envisionment Building in Social Studies/History

Each discipline has its own emphases and ways of considering meaning that derive from the history and particularities of the discipline and that are learned through membership within the larger disciplinary community. In history, Sam Wineburg states, "It is about a way of being—an ontology as much as an epistemology" (personal electronic communication, February 7, 2010).

In the process of enculturation into an academic discipline, students in all subjects learn both particular content knowledge and ways of knowing, doing, and communicating that are accepted as appropriate and necessary for learning and understanding within that particular field. If one goal is to understand the early history of the United States, for example, this means that in addition to deriving a surface understanding of the material, through whatever medium it might have been gained, students must learn to understand and critically analyze the kinds of knowledge that are valued, as well as ways in which evidence is presented and arguments are developed.

It is here that the act of envisionment building plays a critical role. Knowing social studies/history material goes far beyond a literal understanding of information, and involves examining available documents from the various perspectives of the particular people in their particular contexts and their particular times, and constructing a likely understanding of the event in question. This includes the ability to construe and critique it in discipline-appropriate ways as well as the ability to connect it to concepts within the field and world and to generate ideas from it. Recurring envisionment-building experiences, with discipline-appropriate knowledge development as the goal, support students' growing social studies/history literacy.

For example, taking an insider's look at particular points in time and thus questioning the context, point of view, and credibility of sources is a critical social studies/history literacy strategy, since it directly affects how the content will be treated. Perspectives that are taken without regard to the contexts of the time in which they occurred as well as those that have been sanctioned or privileged often lead to interpretations of an issue that are likely different from perspectives that have considered the original context or been marginalized. Therefore, questioning the original context as well as the veracity of sources, gathering data across sources, and understanding the perspectives from which they come are critical reasoning abilities that must be taught and practiced.

In addition to learning to use primary documents and external sources in ways that are appropriate to the discipline, writing about what one knows is also important. The act of writing helps students to gain knowledge as well as to convey it. Thought-provoking writing assignments help students shape their thinking. Through writing, they explore context and veracity of the data, work through the details of connections they make, find ways to make their understandings explicit, and move beyond to deeper understandings. (For greater detail about learning through writing, see Langer, 1986b; Langer & Applebee, 1987.) Writing requires students to arrive at a reasoned understanding both of the material and how to present it in ways that are appropriate to the field. Reading, writing, speaking, and thinking about important issues and questions involve the manipulation of content in ways that help students build richer and more connected envisionments about what they are learning. In doing so, they gain knowledge about the particular course content and about the larger field of social studies/history.

In this chapter, I will point out ways in which a number of the features described in the earlier chapters play out in social studies/history classes. Although all are important, different features will be highlighted in each of the three classroom examples in this chapter. The first example will emphasize the teaching and learning of enabling strategies during envisionment building; the second will highlight the stances that individuals take during envisionment building as a way to provide a closer look at how they work in action; and the third will provide a brief glimpse at sustained discussion in an online format. Before presenting the classroom examples, I will first discuss some current concerns in the field, to provide a lens for thinking about the interweaving relationships between content and literacy in the teaching of social studies/history.

INSTRUCTIONAL FOCI IN SOCIAL STUDIES/HISTORY

A number of studies and articles have identified specific strategies that students need to learn in social studies/history classes. They are central to understanding the material and gaining knowledge as the demands change across the grades. (See, for example, Bransford & Donovan, 2005; Donovan, Wineburg, & Martin, 2004; Langer, 1992a, 1992b, 1994; Shanahan & Shanahan, 2008; Wineburg, 1994, 2005, 2007.) These strategies, which are particularly important in different stances of envisionment building (see Chapter 2), include the following:

- Evaluate sources for the quality of the material before using them. Focus on the author or other source of the information to identify purpose and bias (even with textbooks). Test claims for validity. This involves identifying the position or perspective the work is espousing and consulting other sources to understand alternative perspectives and critically comparing them. Students must also become aware of their own preconceptions. (Stance 4: Thinking Critically)
- Focus on the context as well as the economic, political, social, and cultural factors that are at the core of how the particular era, event, or issue occurred. Understanding history especially involves looking at the multiple perspectives of the people of the times. (Stance 2: Developing Understanding)
- Ask who, what, where, when, how, and why from various vantage points; analyze events for patterns at a particular time and across time. Look for evidence and explanation. Become aware of what you don't know as well as what you do. Use documents to stimulate new questions. (Stance 2: Developing Understanding, Stance 3: Learning from the Material, and Stance 4: Thinking Critically)
- Focus on motivations and biases, consider arguments and points of view from the vantage points of the era, culture, individuals, and circumstances. (Stance 4: Thinking Critically)
- Compare and analyze evidence needed to explain and defend a particular interpretation and provide data to back up interpretations and assertions; give specific evidence and create a sound argument. Explain and elaborate through similarities and contrasts, causes and effects. (Stance 4: Thinking Critically)

- Meaning changes over time. Consider ways in which words as well as actions may have had different meanings during the original events as well as when they were written about at other points in time, when word uses and meanings again may have changed. (Stance 2: Developing Understanding and Stance 4: Thinking Critically)
- Focus on the historic past from a variety of perspectives: Identify, analyze, and connect relationships among people, events, and ideas across time and place (synthesize, generalize, theorize, generate) to note larger issues or themes. (Stance 4: Thinking Critically and Stance 5: Going Beyond)

As Lee (2005) argues, historical knowledge is never unquestionably known; it is subject to change. As knowledge is gained, more questions arise, pointing toward something else that needs to be understood. It is important that students engage with history similarly. The very concept of envisionment building provides an excellent pedagogical frame for this view.

The K–12 curriculum in social studies/history includes a variety of disciplines, including economics, geography, history, and political science. Each of these disciplines has a different set of tools. Each has a particular disciplinary vocabulary, patterns for approaching and solving problems, and ways of providing evidence and organizing oral and written communication. This means that envisionment building in social studies/history needs to be taught through a variety of literate thinking activities that are appropriate to the students, the course, and the various disciplines. When envisionment building is associated with thinking, learning, and communicating about social studies/history issues, it is critical to civic responsibility and daily life as well as to success in social studies/history coursework. Thus, the development of social studies/history literacy becomes a major agenda of instruction for social studies/history teachers.

From this perspective, successful teaching depends in part upon student learning of specific strategies and routines for understanding the information, in part upon the knowledge they build from these in ways that are inextricably linked to advancing knowledge of the content under study, and in part upon the connections they make to other bodies of knowledge within the field, across fields and the world. All are part and parcel of the teaching and learning that occur in the envisioning-building classrooms discussed in Chapter 4. These are minds-on classrooms where teachers encourage envisionment building, help students forge curricular connections, orchestrate substantive discussions, and offer enabling strategies. When the activities engage students in exploring and coming to understand important ideas and issues related to the topics under study, they will practice and learn the critical-thinking strategies that are necessary for gaining knowledge in social studies/history.

A MINDS-ON SOCIAL STUDIES/HISTORY CLASS

Let us look at Karen Polsinelli's 7th-grade social studies class as an example of an envisionment-building classroom. Ms. Polsinelli says that it is very important to have her students learn to think like social scientists. She wants them to examine material from the point of view of the times in which they occurred, to use appropriate vocabulary, ask questions, use data, and present arguments and evidence in the ways that social scientists do. Beginning early in the semester and continuing throughout the year, she asks her class: "What do social scientists need to do?" Soon they answer: "They need to locate, examine, and understand data from four perspectives: political, economic, social, and geographic." From this perspective, Ms. Polsinelli is preparing the students to take a point-of-reference orientation, with the "points" being the particular disciplinary lenses through which they will be expected to sort the information and come to understand and critique the data. She reminds them: "You need to gather the data, analyze it, come to understand it, and ask 'so what?'" Across the year, Ms. Polsinelli has students practice looking at "primary and secondary data" from these perspectives.

Her curriculum for the year is created around "Big Ideas" that she feels are essential to the course of study and to her students' cumulative understanding of the Colonial Era, the American Revolution, and the new country. Ms. Polsinelli treats writing as a tool for learning on a day-to-day basis. She does this within the framework of minds-on teaching: Building envisionments and forging curricular connections are her goals. She uses substantive and engaged discussion and writing, as well as enabling strategies (ways to think and ways to do), as tools to help students develop their knowledge and understanding. In addition to a wide range of shorter writing assignments (e.g., quick writes, small "topic-targeted" think papers, and research reports), which help her students think and learn about the topic, she also has them write four big essays per year, related to the Big Ideas of her curriculum.

Her first unit asks the students to prove that Native Americans had a culture worthy of respect, with a focus on precolonial society. This is followed by units focusing on exploration and colonization. Here, students examine the differing treatment of Native Americans reflected in the initial explorations and colonial policies of France, England, and Spain. The activities are designed to help students gain a deeper understanding of diversity in the colonies, building upon their work in the previous units. Together, the units feed into a later paper on "Was the American Revolution Really a Revolution?"

Each of Ms. Polsinelli's units follows a similar pattern. It begins with a discussion of what the students already know, after which they do research and read the appropriate sections in their textbook as well as a range of other primary and secondary sources, culminating in a larger essay. Thus, the organization of the lessons serves as a scaffold as students build their envisionments of the topic. Along the way, she also guides her students in "ways to think" about the content and "ways to do" the various social studies/history activities. Notice in the descriptions that follow how content, ways of thinking about it, and discipline-appropriate language and structure are continually at the center of her activities and teaching.

Making Connections Overt

When the class is about to start the unit on colonization, Ms. Polsinelli helps the students forge connections between what they had learned before and their new unit. She begins with a question: "What were the effects of contact on the Indians and the Europeans?" Students read from *A History of the U.S.*, by Joy Hakim (2007), which includes an excerpt from a letter written by Columbus describing his first encounter with the Taino. Students had already been gathering information on the European view of contact. To add to their picture of early contact, Ms. Polsinelli shows them the picture book *Encounter* by Jane Yolen (1992), in which the contact experience is viewed through the eyes of a Taino child. Led by Ms. Polsinelli, the students then compare and contrast the Native American and European views that are depicted. Ms. Polsinelli explains why she did this:

> As a transition, to provide a link between units of study and to
> help the students focus on the people and the effects of coloniza-
> tion on the people who were already established in this country.
> Students felt strongly about the effects of contact on the Indians

because they had spent so much time studying them and determining that they were cultures worthy of respect. From there, we began to look at the settlement of the English colonies. American history, especially at 7th grade, can seem very boring to students. By focusing on the people, students were able to feel a connection and have an interest in learning more. I fueled this by giving them opportunities to argue and discuss, and their learning went deeper. I feel the lesson was effective because it helped to keep the point of view of the Indians in their minds as they examined the development of the colonies.

Following her usual routine, almost every lesson begins by looking back at notes, discussion, and review. Students are given time to ask questions and then, as an introduction to new work (building curricular connections), they start with quick writes or journal jots (short reflective notes in response to a teacher's prompt) about the ideas they have in mind about the topic and speculation about what they think they will learn. As her students do research, discuss, and write, Ms. Polsinelli focuses on the kinds of thinking they are doing. In response, she offers enabling strategies as a way to help them think more critically and engage in an ongoing quest to build richer envisionments.

Making Thinking Explicit

For this discussion, we will pick up at the point in her unit where the students are preparing to write a paper on the ways in which the American colonies were diverse. The paper comes after a good deal of research, discussion, and note-taking have taken place. This may seem like an easy question based on all they have already discussed, but Ms. Polsinelli is concerned that her students might not know explicitly what information is pertinent to write about, or how to organize the information they have into meaningful chunks of ideas. She wants them to think and write like social scientists, and also to consider the written form required in an analytic social studies/history paper. Therefore, she offers enabling strategies, both ways to think about the material and ways to do the paper.

She begins with a class discussion about what you need to do to make an analysis and why it is needed for a paper that discusses whether the colonies were diverse or not. The students say they need to examine the data very carefully, looking for causes and effects, similarities and differences, and to give detailed explanations. It is here that Ms. Polsinelli starts to help them think about how to organize their ideas in terms of their assignment—to write an analytic paper on "Diversity in the Colonies."

Ms. Polsinelli: What will we need to think about?

Students: Kinds of diversity; How it affects daily life.

Ms. Polsinelli: Good start—now make two columns:

Diversity / How It Affects Daily Life

Ms. Polsinelli: Is there anything else we'll need to think about? (After no response) Were all the colonies diverse in the same way?

Students: (Murmurs and hands raised) No, there were differences. (Students raise hands to offer some differences.)

Ms. Polsinelli: (She quiets them and asks) How do we group the colonies?

Students: New England, Middle, and Southern.

Ms. Polsinelli: Okay, I'll write it on the Think Chart to remind you that for each column, you need to think three times separately—about diversity in New England, Middle, and Southern colonies. (They write on their charts.)

Ms. Polsinelli: Let's start it together about New England. What do you know about diversity in New England? Look at your notes (from previous days) if it helps ideas come to you.

Students: Religion, only white men could vote, the jobs were different, they lived differently.

Ms. Polsinelli: (She stops them, saying) You have lots of good ideas, but let's see if you can organize them in a way that will help your thinking and your writing. On your Think Chart, for each set of colonies, write the big categories that social scientists need to think about. What are they?

Students: ECONOMIC   POLITICAL   SOCIAL   GEOGRAPHIC

Ms. Polsinelli: (She writes, then says) Geographic, this last, is covered because we are separating them by geographic regions, and that should affect what we're going to write. Let's add these to our Think Charts. When we fill in the chart, first let's think about diversity in the New England colonies. What do we know about ways the economy differed and so on? We do the same thing for each of the three groups of colonies.

They begin to do this together, and when Ms. Polsinelli thinks they have the idea, she asks them to continue on their own, with open notes as she circles the room to help. The next day, she reminds them,

> Remember, we're still working on gathering the evidence we'll need to write a paper on diversity in the colonies, the kinds of diversity, and how it differed across the colonies. Today some of you will be coming really close to having enough data to write your papers. I'll walk around. Ask me questions. Be sure I see your Think Chart before going on.

Figure 5.1 displays Keira's Think Chart, as an example of the work that resulted. Although Keira does not mention either Native Americans or African American slaves in the colonies, it was a topic of discussion in class, and this is pointed out.

Figure 5.1. Keira's Think Chart

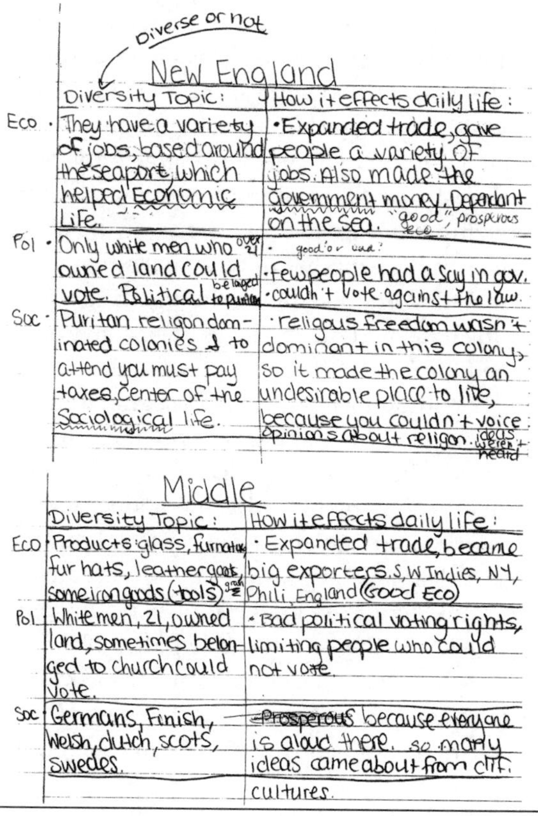

Diverse or not

New England

	Diversity Topic:	How it effects daily life:
Eco	They have a variety of jobs, based around the seaport, which helped Economic Life.	•Expanded trade, gave people a variety of jobs. Also made the government money. Dependant on the sea. "good" eco, prosperous
Pol	Only white men who over 21 owned land could vote. Political belonged to puritan	• good or bad? •Few people had a say in gov. •couldn't vote against the law.
Soc	Puritan religon dominated colonies & to attend you must pay taxes, center of the Sociological life.	•religous freedom wasn't dominant in this colony, so it made the colony an undesirable place to live, because you couldn't voice opinions about religon. ideas weren't heard

Middle

	Diversity Topic:	How it effects daily life:
Eco	Products: glass, furnature fur hats, leathergoods, some iron goods (tools) grain	· Expanded trade, became big exporters. S, W Indies, NY, Phili, England (Good Eco)
Pol	Whitemen, 21, owned land, sometimes belonged to church could vote.	• Bad political voting rights, limiting people who could not vote.
Soc	Germans, Finish, Welsh, dutch, scots, Swedes.	~~Prosperous~~ because everyone is aloud there. so many ideas came about from diff. cultures.

Figure 5.1. Keira's Think Chart *(continued)*

> *Why is this important?*
> *So What?*
>
> Southern
>
> | Diversity Topic: | How it effects daily life: |
> |---|---|
> | Eco • Tobacco was their only cash crop. | • Supply & demand effected the good and bad years of tobacco growing. |
> | Pol • Plantation owners ruled the goverment, they picked who could & couldn't vote. | • Disadvantage to the people who were not rich, bad Political. |
> | Soc • Little education, rich plantation owners hired tutors | • People who weren't rich enough to hire tutors were poorly educated. Bad for Soc |
> | | Why? How? fewer skilled craftsmen, fewer goods made trade, limited ideas to voice |

You can see in these examples that Ms. Polsinelli offers some very important tools for her students to use in order to step into and build richer envisionments about diversity in the colonies. More particularly, she gives them pointers on "ways to think" about the material from the perspective of social studies/history as well as "ways to do." She models how to organize the Think Chart into categories, and then to use those categories to organize and write their papers. She not only engages them in a substantive and sustained discussion and writing activity, but to do so they also need to use almost all the critical-thinking strategies listed in Chapter 4, including analyzing the data to make sense of them and understand them more deeply, synthesizing the data to make them cohere as a unit, evaluating their meaning and usefulness in regard to understanding the topic, explaining the data, and providing evidence that the arguments are data-based and credible.

She also helps her students learn ways to segment the task of writing such a paper, making it more manageable for them to think about the material. In doing so, she helps them learn "ways to do" strategies— ways to select the critical content and write about it in a more mature social studies/history language and form. Throughout the unit, whenever a concept isn't clear, she guides them, individually or collectively, through ways to think about the material or ways to complete the task ("ways to do"). However, she isn't the sole judge. She frequently engages her students in self-reflection. For example, she asks them to respond personally to some questions about the effectiveness of the Think Chart. Here are Keira's written comments in response to the guide questions:

What makes the Think Chart hard?

You have to think big picture, not just with individual lives. This is hard because it is different from how we usually think about things.

How did you solve the problem?

I thought about how the colony would change in a good or bad way without this aspect, and expanded. To expand you have to think about ideas building on other ideas. When you concentrate on this, it makes it easier.

Problems

Based on opinion
Didn't have enough data

Good ideas

Examples
Past vs. today (1750)
Personally vs. community
Write essay & expand on many ideas that can make bigger points

The students then use their Think Charts as a base from which to write their papers. Over the 3 days they do this, there is good discussion and additional scaffolding for individuals as well as the whole class. Ms. Polsinelli asks her students to make comparisons ("Did they treat everyone this way?"), add details ("Where are the data?"), and make judgments ("Why is this a good example of economic diversity and that isn't?"). Throughout, she keeps an eye on their envisionment building, using the class discussions and writing activities as a window into their understandings of the content and the tasks that led to the final written work. Figure 5.2 displays Keira's first draft, with her teacher's comments.

After the students write their first drafts, Ms. Polsinelli asks them to highlight in yellow everything they had written about diversity and to highlight in red everything they had written about the way it had an impact on the people (the two columns on their Think Charts). Then she asks them to use these highlights as a way to check whether they have presented enough data in each of these areas for each of the three sets of colonies. Then they write their final drafts.

Figure 5.2. Keira's First Draft

*= signaled diversity
#= signal of impact

Social Studies   2-5-07

The diversity involved in every day life greatly impacted the New England, middle, and southern colonies. The concept of diversity effected political, economical, and sociological in good and bad ways. *[other words?]*

New England's economy was based around the sea, which gave the working people a variety of jobs. Also this *[delete]* made the economy prosperous in trading with other exporters. In the political aspect of life, only white males, over the age of 21, owned land, and occasionally belonged to the puritan church, *[need a word]* here. condoned. This also means that even though you may disagree with the law, you have no right to vote nor voice your opinion about it. This

gave less opinions to the government, *[less what? what kind?]* which made it difficult to make fair laws, which applied to everyone. concerns Sociological life was very scripted, to which people must belong to the puritan church and follow that religion. This signaled similarities to others, and beliefs about their religion was not discussed. Due to the substantial amount of likeness in the New England colonies, it gave many unfortunate citizens unequal rights. *[is something missing?]*

The Middle colonies were well off in some ways, yet had some downfalls. The economy *[small s]* became big exporters with the South and West Indies, New York, Philidelphia, and England. They traded a variety of *[good]* products including glass, furniture, fur hats, leather goods, and wide iron goods such as

tools. To many people the political system was unjust. Only white males, over the age of 21, who owned land, and occasionally belonged to the puritan church could vote. This was definatly unjust because these *[sp?]* people were not equal. Even though *[treated? and in what way?]* there were many voting restrictions, there were none against the different cultures who moved there. Germans, Finns, Welsh, Scots, dutch, and swedes flooded into the middle colonies, which gave people many opportunities. It gave people opportunities to learn *[what people?]* from and experience ideas that the ethnic groups presented. *[which groups?]*

As an outcome of the diversity in this colony, they gained individiality, which most colonies didn't have.

The southern colonies relied on risky aspects, that resulted into good and bad ways. An example of *[I don't understand]* how these colonies relied on things is that tobacco was their only cash crop. Paired with this is supply of demand among the traders and people of the colony. When the tobacco didn't grow as well as it was supposed to, the price got higher, which made people not want to buy it. When the tobacco had a good & prosperous year, people were encouraged to buy at such a low price. As in all three colonies, the voting rights were unfair to many people. The rich plantation owners literally ruled the government. They picked who could and could not vote, and under no circumstances could you go against them. This gave little opportunity to voice ideas and opinions about the law, which made it difficult to create laws, since laws are infact based on opinion.

Education is important for everyone, but that wasn't the way everybody thought in these colonies. The rich plantation owners hired tutors, and the poor, well, they didn't get educated. This became a big problem because with little education, skilled craftsmen were lacking, which means fewer goods, and shrinking trade. The rich liked these colonies, diversity or not, and because of that they took many risks.

Obviously there was a major lack of diversity in the Middle, New England, and southern colonies. If there was as much diversity as there is today, the colonies would have been far more successful. *[Explain this. You said there was diversity. How different from today.]*

[This is really good information!]

But Ms. Polsinelli is still not done. She wants students to forge curricular connections looking ahead. She says,

Now write your "Ticket Out." Jot down some things you learned during this unit about the data, comparisons, and judgments (that you don't already have in your journal) that you can use when you write your big paper on whether the American Revolution was really a revolution. We always come back to our papers and our notes, so be sure your notes are complete.

Using Rubrics

What I haven't yet mentioned is that before the students began writing the diversity paper, Ms. Polsinelli gave them a rubric to use as a way to plan and evaluate their own writing. She told them that she would later use this rubric in her grading of the papers. Figure 5.3 displays the rubric, with the teacher's comments on Keira's final draft.

Later in the year, Ms. Polsinelli and her students use this rubric to model "ways to do" as they develop new topic-specific rubrics together. Each time, the rubric is used in the same way as it was for the diversity paper. First, students use it to plan what they will write about and how they will organize their papers. After they finish writing, they use the rubric as a way to review what they have written and to make revisions. Next, when they think they are done, they use it to rate themselves before handing in their work. Finally, after Ms. Polsinelli has graded their papers, they compare the two sets of grades. Ms. Polsinelli often has a brief conference with each student, with paper and graded rubric in hand to refer to for specifics.

What the Students Learn

Ms. Polsinelli has an excellent reputation in her school. When her students move on to other social studies/history classes, the new teachers comment on the depth of thinking her ex-students exhibit. The new teachers say they see it not only in the quality of students' discussion and writing, but also in the quality of their thinking about the material—in their ability to gain knowledge and make connections across big ideas, and to grow as social scientists across the years. This sort of envisionment-building class emphasizes discipline-appropriate assignments and activities that have room for students to work at the peak of their abilities while receiving needed help or new challenges from Ms. Polsinelli.

Figure 5.3. The Rubric Applied to Keira's Paper

Unit III: The Founding of New Societies 1607-1763

Question/Problem : In what ways did diversity affect the way of life within the New England, Middle and Southern colonies?

Criteria for Assessment of Diversity Essay

<u>Description</u>: A variety of accurate facts, details and examples used to describe diversity *good data*	Variety of accurate facts, details and examples Sufficient amount of material used to support each region Small amount of supporting information included Little and/or inaccurate information included No supporting data is included	5 ✓ 4 ____ 3 ____ 2 ____ 0 ____
<u>Effect on Life</u>: The effect of diversity on each geographic region is presented *strong analysis*	The effect of diversity on each geographic region is thoroughly explained Three adequate explanations are provided A combination of strong and brief explanations presented Explanations are minimal No attempt made to explain effect of diversity	5 ✓ 4 ____ 3 ____ 2 ____ 0 ____
<u>Organization</u>: Essay follows a clear pattern of organization *closing TP does not follow required format*	Essay follows a clear pattern of organization and includes an introduction and closing Essay is generally organized No organization shown	3 ____ 2 ✓ 1 ____
<u>Writing Style</u>: Essay includes topic sentences and transitions *Watch use of vocab – Sometimes it is clearer if you are to the point*	Clear and readable writing style Readable but some parts are not clear Writing style makes essay difficult to understand	3 ✓ 2 ____ 1 ____ *ex: condone / pertain*
<u>Grammar, Mechanics, Spelling</u>:	Grammar, mechanics, spelling consistently correct Some weaknesses and errors Many errors make reading difficult	2 ✓ 1 ____ 0 ____
<u>Presentation</u> :	Essay proofread and neatly written or typed Sloppy, not neatly presented	1 ✓ 0 ____
<u>Revision</u>:	Rough draft shows evidence of revision No evidence of revision	1 ✓ 0 ____
<u>Timeliness</u>:	Presented when due Late	1 ✓ 0 ____

20-21=A
17-19=B
15-16=C
14=D
<13=U

TOTAL SCORE __+20__

GRADE __A__

An excellent essay. Good development of diversity + its impact on life.

From the perspective of envisionment building, a lot of rich thinking and learning went on in Ms. Polsinelli's classroom of 12-year-olds. She used the minds-on teaching techniques discussed in Chapter 4 to engage her students in deep thinking about their coursework, building envisionments, forging curricular connections, orchestrating substantive and sustained discussion, and offering enabling strategies. Although most of the students' thinking was oriented toward "maintaining a point of reference" (diversity in the colonies, whether the nation met the goals in the Declaration of Independence), they sometimes explored horizons of possibilities when discussing possible connections to the present-day United States or to emerging nations they had been hearing about in the news. Throughout this work, they learned to apply specific critical-thinking strategies in discipline-appropriate ways. Although they are still young students, they are building knowledge of the content and gaining the strategies to continue to do so.

But does this approach work with students who are judged to be struggling learners or those who are in special education classes? Let us look at this, with a focus on how the stances are used to support student envisionment building.

USING THE STANCES IN 8TH-GRADE
SOCIAL STUDIES/HISTORY SPECIAL EDUCATION

Let us look at Laura Carroll and her 8th-grade special education resource class as they do research on the web as part of a unit on imperialism. All the students are also in a regular social studies/history class with heterogeneously grouped students. Ms. Carroll helps them build their envisionments by developing units for her class that engage the students in gaining knowledge about the big ideas underlying the course curriculum. At this point in their regular social studies class, they are working on a unit on the causes of World War I. In the example below, you will see an activity she developed to help the students participate more effectively in their regular class, by broadening their knowledge base about the topic under study. To do this, she helps them engage in point-of-reference thinking in response to her guided questions. Because she wants to help her students learn to approach new content as thoroughly as possible, she developed a set of activities that helped them consider the content from the various stances in envisionment building.

Her students' end product is to write a web-based CultureGram of a particular country or area affected by the imperialism of the United States. The selections were China, Japan, Alaska, and Cuba, and each of the students could choose one. Because of the students' limited experience in doing research on the web, as well as their limited knowledge of the topic, Ms. Carroll confines their research base to the information they could find on the CultureGrams website (www.culturegrams.com) and in their textbook. As a first step, to help the students begin stepping into an envisionment, she invites the social studies/history teacher into her special education classroom to discuss the task, materials, and some background content.

To help the students continue to build initial envisionments, Ms. Carroll begins with background discussions of both imperialism and the countries the students are going to research. To support their envisionment building, the students have opportunities to ask questions, explain and provide evidence for their ideas, and agree and disagree with one another, in each case telling why. As the unit progresses, these discussions are increasingly more substantive and sustained. She then asks her students to read along as they listen to a CD recording of a related text section. Each student is also given a CD to take home to prepare for the class discussion to follow. Since all of the students read far below grade level, she uses this technique as a way to maximize their ability to become familiar with the content and specialized vocabulary, prepare for reading they will later do alone, and be ready to focus on new information they have not yet discussed. In class, the CD is played in segments, so the students can ask questions and raise ideas for discussion.

The Idea Catcher

Ms. Carroll wants to provide even more scaffolding before her students move on to do the CultureGram research. She feels that even when they are exposed to the material, they are uncertain what to focus on, and they give equal weight to almost everything. To help them "make sense" of the material, and become more selective about important and substantiating data, she wants to engage them in moving through the envisionment-building stances (see Chapter 2). To do this, Ms. Carroll has developed an "Idea Catcher" to use as a discussion starter with the class. The "Idea Catcher" is a sheet of paper folded origami-style into a "hat" that opens in four corners. Each open corner lists questions, based on one of the first four stances, for the students to think about and discuss (see Figure 5.4). Each student is given an Idea Catcher and, when asked by Ms. Carroll, opens it to a section, reads a question based on a particular stance, and leads the group in a discussion of the question raised.

Figure 5.4. The Idea Catcher

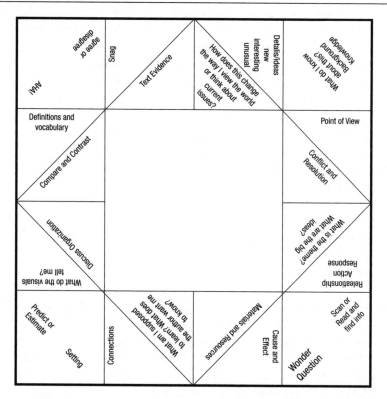

For this unit on imperialism, Ms. Carroll fine-tuned some of the questions as a way to help students focus on particular important issues they are learning about:

- What am I supposed to learn? (Stance 1: Getting Started)
- What do I know about imperialism already? (Stance 1: Getting Started)
- What does the author want me to know about imperialism? (Stance 4: Thinking Critically)
- What are some details/new or interesting ideas? (Stance 2: Developing Understanding)
- What connections can I make? (Stance 2: Developing Understanding)
- What cause and effect do I see? (Stance 2: Developing Understanding and Stance 4: Thinking Critically)

- How does what I read change the way I think about U.S. relations with some other parts of the world? (Stance 4: Thinking Critically)
- What is my wonder question about imperialism? What is the big idea about imperialism? (Stance 1: Getting Started, Stance 2: Developing Understanding, and Stance 5: Going Beyond)
- What is my evaluation of U.S. imperialism in the country I selected, pros and cons? (Stance 4: Thinking Critically)

Note that more than one stance applies to a question when there are different ways a student might approach and respond to the question.

Ms. Carroll uses this activity at various points in the unit as a way to ensure that the students are deepening their envisionments by considering the topic from a variety of stances. The questions engage the students in discussion about imperialism and its motives and effects, and encourage them to look at the material from the vantage points captured by the stances.

Research on the Web

One big focus in the imperialism unit asks the essential question, "How did the United States achieve its status as an imperialist nation?" To help students address this, Ms. Carroll engages them in doing research on the CultureGrams website in addition to reading their text, with support.

For the web-based CultureGrams activity, she gives the students a set of guiding questions to focus their search. They are to gather data and take notes, plan, and then write about U.S. relations with their focus country over time. The envisionment-building activities they have done with stances have helped prepare the students to do this independently. As they work, Ms. Carroll differentiates instruction by helping each student separately, using the stances as a guide to determine the extent of their envisionments and the kind of support needed to help them move beyond. For example, for a student who is experiencing more difficulty than the others in beginning to build an envisionment, she reduces the task by limiting the assignment and asking guiding questions about the information on which he will focus. She also helps the student make judgments about the usefulness of the specific information.

To help students keep their "minds in motion" as they continue to build upon their envisionments, Ms. Carroll models, guides, and supports as they learn to navigate the culturegrams.com website and make decisions about the kinds of information that are relevant to the question at hand. Figure 5.5 provides an abbreviated copy of the assignment.

Figure 5.5. The CultureGrams Assignment

IMPERIALISM

Big Conversation: Challenges and Change

Essential Question: How did the United States achieve its status as an imperialist nation?

Name_____ Date_____

Task: Create a CultureGram of a country or area affected by U.S. imperialism. MAKE A STATEMENT about how the United States changed its relationship with this area or country.

Choose a country or area (only one person per country or state): China, Japan, Alaska, or Cuba.

Log on to: http//online.culturegrams.com/index.php. You will get your information from this website.

1. List three meaningful facts about your country or area.

2. Give a summary of the climate and land formations.

3. What is the population?

4. What is the major language? Name two interesting facts about the language.

5. What is the major religion? Name two interesting facts about this religion.

6. Find two important dates in the history after 1900, and tell why.

13. What type of government is there? Who is the leader? What is that position called?

14. What type of money is used? Find two interesting facts about money.

16. Describe social customs of this country or area.

20. Name and tell about one famous person from this country or area.

21. Use the CultureGram website or your textbook to find how this country was affected by U.S. imperialism. Take notes as you read. When you are done with your notes, make a statement about how this country was affected by U.S. imperialism.

As you see, the questions in this assignment scaffold the work by providing a structured set way for the students to approach the CultureGrams website. (This is similar to the structuring of ways to think and ways to do that Ms. Polsinelli offered in the earlier example.) Look at questions 1–5. You will see that they help the students gain a very general introduction to the country. They offer support for students to move through Stance 1 (Getting Started) and begin developing envisionments about the country or area they have selected. Now look at questions 6–20. Here, we see students being asked to consider issues of culture, history, and government in their country as a way to help them think through Stance 2 (Developing Understanding) and even Stance 3 (Learning from the Material). In this class, there is considerable envisionment building even before the students consider issues of imperialism.

Here is Sonya's definition of imperialism, from her CultureGrams.

Imperialism is wen a plas taks up, anexis or controls sevrul diferint plaseis all at woons and they do it for traed, pawer, to macke an epiyer, control and for other reasons.

[Imperialism is when a place takes up, annexes, or controls several different places all at once and they do it for trade, power, to make an empire, control, and for other reasons.]

Clearly, through these activities, she has gained both content knowledge and vocabulary.

Now look at question 21. It is a big one. It is the one the social studies teacher and Ms. Carroll are really after. Ms. Carroll feels that her students need to develop the other understandings before confronting this question. Now they are asked to advance interpretations of information that are not always directly stated in their source material. They have to end with their own statement about how their focus country was affected by U.S. imperialism.

After the students complete their writing, they participate in discussions where they present what they found, ask questions, compare countries or regions, and try to identify specific features that had contributed to imperialism. This last discussion points toward a larger essay on imperialism that the students will later write for Ms. Carroll.

After the students had completed their CultureGrams activity, they participated in a jigsaw activity (in response to teacher questions) in their regular social studies class. The questions, for each of the four countries studied, were: How did we acquire it? What is our relationship with the country today? Ms. Carroll's students participated comfortably with their classmates in this activity and offered thoughtful and sometimes new content that was helpful for all to consider. When speaking informally with Ms. Carroll about her students, the social studies teacher said, "Sonya is on FIRE! Come show me what you did with them when you get the chance."

ONLINE DISCUSSION IN A
HIGH SCHOOL WORLD HISTORY CLASS

In the two examples so far, the teacher plays an active role in the lesson, albeit with a focus on fostering students' ability to envision and develop knowledge. But in minds-on classes, students' envisionments can also grow when they engage in substantive and sustained discussion with one another, when the teacher's role is minimal. Let us look at Ms. Snyder's world history class to see one way this can happen. She begins with a point-of-reference assignment to engage the students in the following electronic discussion:

> Based on your reading of Chapter 22 and your class notes, do you believe that the causes of the French Revolution were primarily economic or primarily political? Explain your response using examples to support your argument. You must respond first by giving your point of view. Then, revisit the discussion three more times on three different days to contribute to your group's conversation.

This assignment is meant to invite students to engage in ongoing envisionment building while forging curricular connections. She uses technology as a tool for engagement in substantive and sustained discussion. The students are also given a political cartoon in an attempt to help them focus on the issues. All electronic discussions take place outside the classroom, and each posting is to be at least three or four sentences long. In addition, students are to use a discussion rubric (also used for in-class discussions) to score themselves based on their participation. All students participate, although a few make only three as opposed to four postings. (Daily class sessions engage the students in discussing, writing about, and doing research on various aspects of their French Revolution unit, of which the electronic discussion is a part.)

As you will see from the selection from their online postings below, students are engaged with the content and stay focused on the discussion question and their developing response.

Hester: If you were to ask me, "was the French Revolution primarily political or economic," my first reaction would be both. However, upon more extensive research and further reflection, I find that I lean more towards the economic side of this debate. [She goes on with historical facts to support her view.] . . .

Rachel: In light of Hester's response, I'd have to say that I respectfully disagree. Although there were many issues dealing with France's economy during revolutionary times, the political spectrum dominated many people's feelings of rebellion. [She follows with historical examples.] . . .

Jeremy: I'm going to have to side with Hester on her opinion that it was primarily economic factors that caused the French Revolution. I do agree with everyone who is saying that the government was the major cause of the economic problems. But . . . for those of you who support the opinion that the revolution was caused for political reasons, what could the government at the time have done to fix the problems of France?

Not only do the students pick up on particular comments and give appropriate examples, but they also leave room for others to react or reply. Sometimes their posts serve as models of "ways to think" about the content or "ways to do" the written presentation. Thus, the students can learn from one another. Because the quality of the student comments is high, a range of issues is discussed, with students being challenged to consider some that have not occurred to them.

The teacher also expects them to make use of the cognitive strategies necessary for high-level discussion (see Chapter 4). These are captured in the discussion rubric and ensure that the students engage with the content in analytic, generative, and evaluative ways. In doing this, they also need to hone their understandings of disciplinary vocabulary, write clearly expressed opinions, and offer discipline-appropriate evidence. In these ways, Ms. Snyder said, the students worked together to advance their own as well as their classmates' knowledge.

SUMMING UP

In envisionment-building social studies/history classes like those of Ms. Polsinelli, Ms. Carroll, and Ms. Snyder, students begin by thinking about their own envisionments, but they soon go beyond, learning from the range of material at their disposal as well as from the many thought-provoking activities and discussions in which they participate. They use their interactions with others to provoke new ideas and investigations. They maintain points of reference as they search for data, question and test its veracity as well as relevance, and make judgments and interpretations. Although each of the teachers uses a wide range of approaches, including direct instruction and careful scaffolding, the students bear responsibility for their own developing understandings. They are guided in ways to become literate thinkers in social studies/history, using language and form as well as content that are appropriate to the discipline.

Further, you can see that envisionment-building classrooms are cognitively active and personally exciting places where students are truly engaged with the ideas at hand and where they thoroughly enjoy their quest to know more. What makes this happen? Part of it comes from the nature of the classwork and part from the nature of the teaching. The classwork is always planned around activities that bring the students into direct confrontation with data for them to examine, analyze, and make judgments about, and it is sequenced in a manner that builds on students' growing understandings, moving them to use what they are learning in ways that add to their knowledge. The teaching is interactive, with students' voices as commonly heard as the teacher's. The teacher gives students guidance in ways to think about the material as well as ways to carry out the assignments in discipline-appropriate ways. Together, the activities help students examine and analyze data from the perspectives of the past, and make connections about their understandings of that past to its relevance for the present.

All three classes discussed in this chapter provided students with content as well as strategies to gain information, and also to consider it within the larger context of social, cultural, and historical sense. The teachers' approaches exemplified the four features of the envisioning knowledge classroom: building envisionments, forging curricular connections, orchestrating substantive and sustained discussion, and offering enabling strategies. In the next chapter, we will explore how this sort of envisionment-building classroom is carried out in science classes.

CHAPTER 6

Envisionment Building in Science

A naive view of science assumes that science content knowledge is unquestionably stable—to do science requires an acceptance of established scientific facts and that is what teachers must see that their students learn. In reality, specialists in the field of science have long talked about the instability of knowledge and the need for critical inquiry (Langer, 1992b; Langer & Applebee, 1988). Nonetheless, the closer to the daily classroom activities of the student as opposed to the ideas in the field, the more the focus seems to turn to facts, to the exclusion of ways to think about them, question them, or see them as other than inviolable and unaffected by context. There are two components of academic learning in science, one having to do with content, the other having to do with ways of knowing and doing that are considered appropriate and necessary for learning, understanding, and participating in a particular scientific field (Langer, 1992a, 1994).

From the envisionment-building perspective, the teaching of the sciences involves helping students engage in appropriate scientific inquiry; it is directly related to apprenticing students into ways of knowing and doing within the field. It involves giving students opportunities to move beyond their preconceptions and misconceptions by engaging in activities that are appropriate to the various sciences, such as making observations; generating questions; developing their own experiments; building functional models; making interpretations; seeking explanatory, corroborating, or conflicting evidence; making conceptual connections; and recording and reporting their work. The focus here is not merely on problem-solving, but on students' use of appropriate scientific knowledge in the act of problem-solving, with conceptual understanding as the goal. The acquisition of knowledge plays an important role, but so does disciplinary reasoning. These highly literate activities are at the heart of learning in the various fields of science. They provide students with opportunities to learn not only what, but how scientists know (e.g., Donovan & Bransford, 2005; Lehrer, Carpenter, Schauble, & Putz, 2000; Schauble, 1996). These activities are also at the heart of envisionment building in science and in the minds-on classroom that supports its development.

WHAT AND HOW SCIENTISTS KNOW

The field of science education has been strongly influenced by the notion of experience and discovery at the heart of science instruction (e.g., American Association for the Advancement of Science, 1993; Brown, Collins, & Draguid, 1989; Latour, 1990). From this perspective, class activities cognitively engage students in setting questions, exploring possibilities, developing points of reference, and finding ways to seek answers. They invite students to engage in envisionment-building activities as ways to dig beneath the surface of science—to explore, ask, and answer appropriate and substantive questions; to critically analyze and evaluate data and interpretations; to reach conclusions; to act upon what they have learned; and to go beyond it.

Lemke (1990) argues that there is a specialized language of science. Since science teachers are already part of the scientific community where such language is in use, it is their role to help students enter the community. To do this, science classrooms must become learning communities where science content, vocabulary, ways of thinking, and forms of expression are taught and practiced in everyday activities. Science classrooms, then, act as critical contexts for students' growing envisionments and literate thinking in science (see, for example, Greenleaf, Schoenbach, Cziko, & Mueller, 2001; Langer, 1992b; Shanahan & Shanahan, 2008). Through experience and instruction, students learn science literacy abilities such as the following:

- To transform information from one form to another (e.g., from observations to graphs, charts, models, or visual representations)
- To look for patterns and relationships
- To categorize and classify
- To unpack and describe processes and procedures
- To relate what they see to principles they already know and to identify potential conflicts

- To take notes, summarize findings, and write reports in a scientific manner (using field-appropriate vocabulary, argument, and evidence)
- To convincingly communicate their questions, challenges, and findings to others in their science community

In their learning, students engage primarily in point-of-reference thinking and enter the various stances from this orientation. They learn to critique existing knowledge and seek the new.

Further, McCommas (1996) argues that scientists in different fields have different methods; that there is no fixed sequence of steps, but rather, a plurality of methods. From this perspective, science-appropriate methods do not provide a recipe, but rather suggest sets of processes—ones that at their best involve envisionment building in the kinds of minds-on environments described in Chapter 4. When envisionment building is associated with thinking about, learning, and communicating in the sciences, it brings the science into the knowledge base of students who learn to understand appropriate scientific principles, properties, and behaviors; apply them in new contexts in their further studies; and generate new applications throughout their lives. Thus, the development of literate thinking in the various fields of science, achieved through multiple acts of envisionment building, becomes a major agenda of instruction for science teachers.

Successful science teaching thus depends in part upon student learning of specific strategies and routines for understanding information, in part upon the knowledge they build using these strategies to advance knowledge of the content under study, in part upon the connections they make to other bodies of knowledge within the field and in their environments, and in part upon their ongoing curiosity and ingenuity. All can be achieved through the teaching and learning that occur in envisionment-building classrooms. These are minds-on classrooms where teachers encourage students to explore horizons of possibilities as well as maintain points of reference. They are classes where teachers encourage envisionment building, help students forge curricular connections, orchestrate substantive discussions, and offer enabling strategies. When the activities engage students in exploring and coming to understand important ideas and issues related to the topics under study, they will practice and learn the critical-thinking strategies that are necessary for gaining knowledge in science.

The classroom examples that follow illustrate ways in which all the features discussed in Chapters 1–4 come into play in science classes in action. However, I will focus in particular in these examples on the use of substantive and sustained discussion and writing to build scientific understandings, including an understanding of the technical language and forms of argument and evidence that are appropriate to discourse in a field of science.

AN 8TH-GRADE SCIENCE CLASS:
SUSTAINED DISCUSSION AND WRITING ABOUT EXPERIMENTS

Let us look at Monica Judd's 8th-grade class as an example of a knowledge-building classroom. Ms. Judd says it is of utmost importance that her students learn to become critical thinkers in science. Across the year, she helps them build envisionments as they forge curricular connections as well as real-world connections. To do this, she orchestrates substantive and sustained discussion and writing as ways for the students to think through and become more familiar with the content and language. She has them make observations, apply the concepts they already know, ask questions about the phenomena under study, make hypotheses from the known to the new, conduct experiments to test their hypotheses, and be alert for corroborating or disconfirming evidence that they then analyze for explanations. In doing this, she creates activities that invite both horizons-of-possibilities and point-of-reference thinking.

Ms. Judd begins her year with a series of lessons that review science processes and reinforce safety, while also introducing concepts of molecules and pressure—essential concepts that students will continue to build upon throughout the year. She treats discussion and writing as tools for learning on a day-to-day basis. As part of a mid-September series of lessons on air pressure, the students investigate condensation through the Soda Can experiment, in which a soda can filled with water is brought to a boil and then plunged into ice water. The question is, what will happen and why? At this point, students have already seen and discussed introductory experiments demonstrating how heat affects the movement of molecules and are conceptually prepared for this next experience.

The minds-on experiment is organized around observation, analysis, discussion, writing, explanation, evidence, and reflection. Ms. Judd feels that when science processes are applied to highly engaging experiments, all students can be challenged to think about, understand, and learn about molecules and pressure—even the three special education students who are mainstreamed into this class. Together, the students discuss what they are going to do, develop the hypothesis they are going to test, and write this as a journal jot. Here, they all are challenged to find appropriate language with which to express their ideas both orally and in writing. Most students hypothesize that bubbles will come out of the can and rise to the surface. As the experiments (done in groups) begin, they are keen observers, taking notes and also discussing what they see occurring each step of the way. Many of their prior envisionments are challenged and they need to reinspect the outcome of the experiment and rethink their hypotheses. Ms. Judd encourages student discussion so they can collectively try to make sense of what occurred and to find language to express it.

The soda cans are heated to boiling, then plunged into ice-cold water. After seeing the cans implode, the students discuss their observations and initial explanations within their own group and with the other groups. Once again, they engage in substantive and sustained discussion as a way to refine their envisionments as they work toward a more fully thought-through description of what happened. Then they individually write a Soda Can Reflection (for 20 points) and informally discuss their ideas with other groups. Here is part of the discussion that followed these activities:

Ms. Judd: The reason I wanted you to see what other groups were saying was to question, "What's the evidence?" So?

Paul: Temperature of the water

Julia: Boiling water—room temperature

Ms. Judd: Support by evidence

Ryan: Bubbles coming up because air (inaudible)

Ms. Judd: Excellent perception. Are there any other theories in your head? I want you to think about it objectively. Think of the evidence. Make connections outside the lab that this reminds you of.

Kevin: Heat and cold reaction

Here, Ms. Judd provides a strategy that emphasizes ways to think, asking students to connect evidence to real-world occurrences and use this to search for explanations.

Michele: Cold water in my hands and then with hot water it hurts
Ryan: Like an ice cube cracking when it hits warm water
Ms. Judd: In conclusion, the soda can collapsed because. . . .

Here is Ms. Judd's assignment, asking the students to reflect on their experiments. She uses the questions to structure what they should be thinking about.

Soda Can Reflection

Using what you've learned through observation, contemplation, and discussion, write a reflection that shares your ideas about why the soda cans collapsed. As you write, be sure to support your ideas with evidence in the form of observations that were made during the lab or connections to related things you have observed elsewhere.

1. Was the original hypothesis supported by the evidence? (2 pts)
2. Why did the cans collapse? Use evidence from the lab to help explain. Also include examples from other groups where appropriate. (10 pts)
3. How do the cans' reactions compare to other real-life phenomena? (5 pts)
4. Summarize the conclusion reached in one or two sentences. (3 pts)

Think scientifically and write objectively.

This assignment offers enabling strategies by pointing out ways to think about the experiment as well as ways to engage in this kind of scientific reporting (by specifying the parts to write about, step-by-step). Writing, student feedback, and revision are integral to the science learning experience. The assignment also engages students in using writing heuristics (Keys, Hand, Prain, & Collins, 1999) as a way to make classroom activity more like "real science." In this way, she is using the minds-on classroom as a forum for the appropriation of a specialized language and legitimate forms of science writing.

When they are finished, the students discuss their findings and interpretations with each other, reflect on what they have written, rethink their explanations, and write a second draft. Then they exchange their papers with another student in their group, and write comments and questions. Still Ms. Judd is inviting their envisionments to continue to grow. When one student reads, "For example, like when you're taking a hot cup out of the dishwasher and getting a really cold drink, it sometimes cracks," he writes, "Good example. I never thought of it." When another student writes, "On the other hand, the cold water on the outside has tightly packed molecules making it stronger," the reviewer writes, "Good scientific language." When the papers are returned to their writers, the students discuss their comments and reactions with one another in their groups, as Ms. Judd walks from group to group, helping them focus on content, language, and form. Notice how often the students have had opportunities to present their growing understandings, to discuss and explain them in discussion and writing, and then to reflect on and revise them—all while focusing on how as well as what to say in science.

A Focus on Language and Content

It is interesting to note that after one student uses the word *implode* during class discussion, it becomes incorporated into the class vocabulary, used by others in conversation as well as in their writing. Let's look at the beginning of Carmel's second draft, with the comments of another student in her work group written into the margins. Carmel is an average student, as is her classmate. The example in Figure 6.1 is typical of her classmate's feedback to the entire draft, either pointing out structural problems in light of the purpose of the report or offering specific scientific, procedural, or activity-based information she felt needed to be explicated.

Carmel takes the comments quite seriously, asks a few questions, and, using a computer, writes a more comprehensive and well-organized final draft. Notice how much more knowledge (beyond the procedures) she shares now that she understands what is appropriate and needed for her report. The request for explanations and evidence helps her write a more complete report that demonstrates what Carmel understands, and also provides visible evidence to Ms. Judd of what concepts need refining. Excerpts are below:

The Soda Can Lab

During the expirament, the original hypothesis was not supported by the evidence. The original hypothesis was that the can and the water containing inside the can would be very hot. In reaction the

Figure 6.1. The Beginning of Carmel's Second Draft

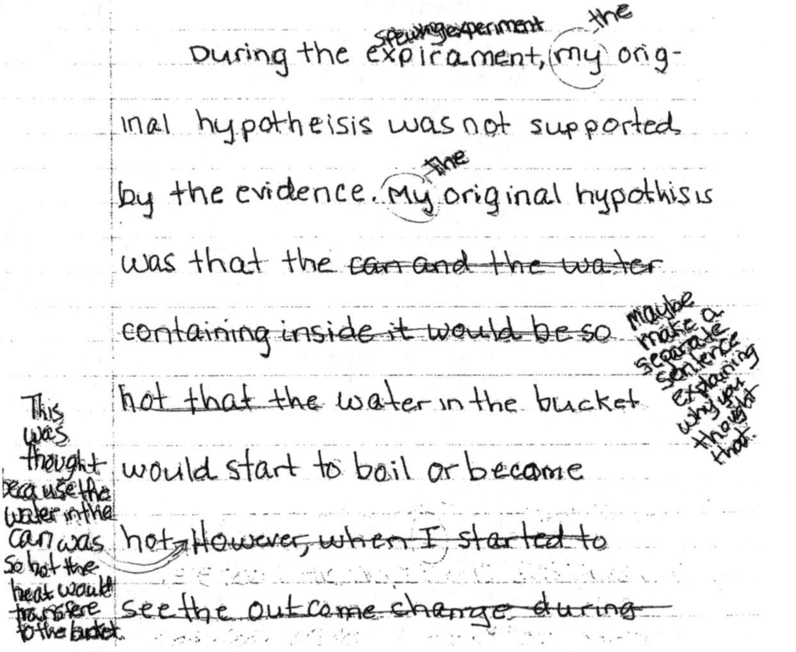

water in the bucket would start to boil or become hot like the can. This was thought because. . . . Using the outcome of the experiment a second hypothesis was developed: This was that the can would expand or shrink in reaction to the cold water.

The soda cans collapsed because the water molecules inside the can were moving very fast, and in the bucket the molecules were just floating around. When the molecules were mixed together, the cold molecules started to move very fast around the can, and as a result, the water inside the can forced its way out because there was no room for the hot water. . . .

The cans' reaction reminds me of when you mix warm water with ice, the ice crackles, and also when you pour noodles in a pot of boiling water, the water fizzles and then goes back to boiling. . . .

In conclusion, the soda can collapsed because of the amount of water, the temperature of the water, and the water molecules.

In comparison, Eric is a struggling reader who told us he was being asked to do more writing in science class than ever before. He does not participate much in discussions, but he listens well and sometimes asks questions. He likes doing the experiments. Figure 6.2 displays Eric's second draft in its entirety, with his group members' comments.

As you can see, the feedback from Eric's classmates asks for particular kinds of additional content information (e.g., details and examples, explanations) that Eric can provide, as well as suggestions about the structure appropriate to this report. Although his word-processed final draft is not much longer, it shows that he tries to be responsive to the reviewers' comments. It also points to specific areas of need for Ms. Judd to follow up on.

The evidence did not support the original Hypothesis. Instead Of
the can melting the can collapsed. The can collapsed because of
The boiling hot can go quickly into the ice-cold water resulting in
The air presser forcing the can in. Like a Cold ice Cube into warm
water makes the ice cube crack Because of the temperature drop. I

Figure 6.2. Eric's Second Draft

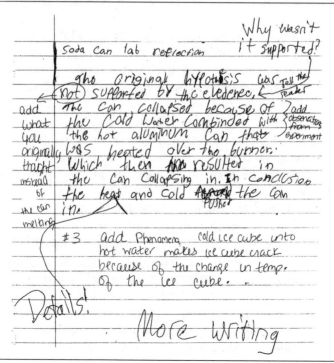

also observed that dropping the can into the water and slamming the can Into the water has an impact. Slamming doesn't push the can in as much as dropping the can into the water.

Last is an example of the final draft written by Manny, a special education student who was mainstreamed into Ms. Judd's science class.

> The original hypothesis was not right. Because the original was that the can was just going to splash water up. When the hot can went in the water it just crumpled. So when the hot goes to cool it smashed.
>
> The reason why the can clasped is the oxygen in side and the water was starting to boil. So all of the oxygen in the can was evaporating so when the hot can went on the cool water it just pushed the sides of the cans in. so it was because of the water in side the can and the cool water out side.
>
> The real life thing was that when you put a hot pane in cool water it cracks. Those are the real life things.
>
> So this is what I thought when the water can smashed.

As you can see, although Manny may have a slightly better understanding of the science than Eric, he has less understanding of the appropriate language and structure called for in the report. This information is particularly helpful in follow-up by both Ms. Judd and Manny's instructional aide.

Later in this unit, as a homework assignment, Ms. Judd asks the students to explain to their parents why it is possible to boil water in a flask without reaching 100 degrees centigrade, as a way to give them practice in thinking about and explaining the concepts underlying an experiment they had done in class.

During work time, the students in Ms. Judd's class are minds-on. Despite their diverse backgrounds and knowledge, they all have room to learn beyond what they already know. Ms. Judd gives them ample time to engage in substantive and sustained discussion and writing about the topic they are studying as they are building envisionments and forging curricular connections. Even struggling readers and special education students are able to exhibit what they know and to learn from others' comments. All gained from discussing and defending their ideas and hearing others' language, as well as from students' and teachers' comments on their work.

Exploring States of Matter

When introducing a later unit on the classification of matter, Ms. Judd begins by asking her students to read an article on alchemy. She does this to provide them with some perspective on how scientific concepts have changed over time. Then the students apply a solution that turns their pennies a golden color. This becomes the basis for a discussion on alchemy and states of matter, as well as physical properties of matter.

Ms. Judd helps her students reason about changing states of water, both boiling water and filtered water, in the context of the next experiment they are going to do. Ms. Judd says, "Yesterday you looked at salt and sand that you had separated. Today let's see what happens if you take the filtrate in your vial and boil away the water instead of letting the water evaporate." (The word *filtrate* had appeared in the procedures for their lab, but when Ms. Judd mentioned it during their experiment, while pointing to the liquid that was left after the salt and sand were filtered out, they began to use it on their own.) "Write what you expect to happen and draw what you expect to see. Afterward, you'll write what you actually saw and try to explain why." As before, here we see Ms. Judd helping students focus on language—on how to express what they see as well as on the appropriate scientific vocabulary.

After much discussion, the next day the students read the procedures for the lab and, with some safety pointers from Ms. Judd, begin their experiments. When they finish, Ms. Judd asks them about what they have seen.

Eric: It was black and deformed a lot.
Ms. Judd: How does it differ from the salt you saw yesterday?
Lydia: Shape changed and it was light
Carmen: Maybe it burned together. . . .
Ms. Judd: (as class was ending) Look at the particles without the
    light.
Paul: They look like clouds in the sky.

The next day, on a video screen, she shows them a sample of what they had seen.

Ms. Judd: Yesterday you saw crystals. You said some were
    monstrous. Now look at them.

Julia: Not linear

Ms. Judd: Why do you think they look different?

Frank: Maybe it took more time so it came out differently.

Betty: Things dissolve in a different way from when they are heated.

Carl: Boiling gets rid of the salt and heat makes it conglomerate.

Ms. Judd: Maybe heat, maybe time. . . . I won't know you know the difference until you learn the terminology. Let's talk about heterogeneous and homogeneous mixtures. Also, see page 67 in your lab book. It will help.

Students read and discuss until the concepts are clearer. Then they write their reports, share them, and update both their thinking and their writing. Both the discussion and their writing have helped shape their envisionments as well as moved their understandings along.

What Students Are Learning

In Ms. Judd's minds-on class, there is room for envisionments to be developed and refined. In response to Ms. Judd's efforts to have students engage in substantive and sustained discussion and writing, the students' comments are thoughtful, and ways to analyze, support, and make connections to larger concepts in science and life are reinforced. Further, their science vocabulary and the meanings those words carry continue to grow over time. In each case, with Ms. Judd's scaffolding, students become more scientifically accurate. Their envisionments of scientific concepts grow, and they become better able to engage in literate thinking within a scientific domain.

THINKING CRITICALLY IN A HIGH SCHOOL PHYSICS CLASS

Andres Harris* similarly focuses on the importance of substantive and sustained conversation with the students in his physics class. He wants his students not only to learn the content in their textbooks, but also to be able to think critically about the different perspectives that scientists have taken. For example, in his unit on climate change and global warming, he shows his class two films with contrasting viewpoints, *An Inconvenient*

Truth (2006) and *The Great Global Warming Swindle* (2007). The views of global warming presented in the two films are almost diametrically opposed, although both are based on a variety of scientific data. This extreme difference of opinion has an electrifying effect on the students and, as Mr. Harris had hoped, leads to enlivened envisionment-building discussion. Mr. Harris says, "The students were pretty much shaken up in a good way, the rest of the semester!" The students immediately understand their need to learn more about the topic, to develop and strengthen their own points of view with credible facts, and to be able to bolster their argument against an opposing point of view.

The students begin with a lengthy discussion and critique of the films' content, exploring what they understand each perspective to be and examining the evidence that was used to substantiate it. Mr. Harris then asks the students to read and take notes on what they learn from three website searches, and to be ready to discuss the perspectives each takes as well as the nature and veracity of the evidence presented. The sites are "What Is Global Warming?" from Wikipedia, http://en.wikipedia.org/wiki/Global-warming; "The Controversy over Global Warming" from Wikipedia, http://en.wikipedia.org/wiki/Global-warming-controversy; and "The Discovery of Global Warming" from the American Institute of Physics, http://www.aip.org/history/climate/.

Here, we see the students engaged in envisionment building through extended discussion of controversial material, with Mr. Harris offering ways to think about what they read and see. These activities move the students through a number of the stances in envisionment building, but put particular emphasis on the fourth (Thinking Critically About the Material).

After the students study these sites, they have a lengthy discussion not only of the points of views and evidence given, but also of how to recognize evidence that is more likely to be scientifically based. The students are then told to select and read a book on global warming and to write a book review of it to present to the class. Mr. Harris participates in the assignment, reading and presenting a book review of his own. The careful readings, analyses, and discussions throughout the unit inevitably involve the students in their own personal searches for evidence that they consider convincing. While they learn a lot about global warming, they also learn a lot about the need to consider differing perspectives, the need for critical inquiry, the need to question and critique the information presented, and the need to search for additional evidence on their own.

This last experience moves the students to new levels of curricular connections and topic understanding as well as language use. They have moved from the first stance (Getting Started with the Material), through the second stance (Developing Understanding of the Material), and into the fourth stance (Thinking Critically About the Material). Over time, they have gained sufficient knowledge of the topic, as well as what is considered compelling evidence in science, to become critics of what they read.

SUMMING UP

In envisionment-building classes such as Ms. Judd's and Mr. Harris's, students learn scientific concepts and language and learn to think and reason in science. Students begin by thinking about their own envisionments, but because of their many opportunities for investigation, discussion, reading, and writing, they soon go beyond their own understandings, learning from the range of material and ideas at their disposal. They maintain points of reference as they search for data, set and test hypotheses, and make judgments and interpretations. The nature of the particular activities in which they engage is based on the particular science course they are taking and the language and rules of thought that are associated with it. Biology, chemistry, physics, and earth science are located within different discourse communities, and how students learn to think, speak, and write about the disciplinary content is as important as the specific content they learn. In the envisionment-building classroom, students' understandings build and change over time, and their knowledge of language as well as content grows.

In these classes, students begin by reflecting on their own envisionments but they soon go beyond, learning from provocative hands-on and minds-on experiences with data. Further, they use their interactions with their classmates as well as their own writing to help them think critically about what they are studying. They are led to reflect on, question, and defend their understandings and assumptions. They also learn to think, explain, and structure communications in scientifically appropriate ways.

Over time, students become increasingly self-reflective, resourceful, and successful critical thinkers as they become enculturated into the ways of thinking and doing that are appropriate to the particular field of science.

When they "don't get it," they are helped to think through what went wrong and how they can think about or do it differently. They are also encouraged to try things out. They are guided to become literate thinkers in science. Discussion, writing, reading, and attention to language and structure are consistently treated as part of the complex of science content. It is the interrelationship between content and literacy that helps students' knowledge and understanding of science to grow. Across the school year and across their years at school, students move from particular instances to more general principles and back, build more complex concepts about content and language, and in doing so are apprenticed into the science community.

CHAPTER 7

Envisionment Building
in Mathematics

The Third International Mathematics and Science Study (Kelly, Mullis, & Martin, 2000) suggests that mathematics instruction in the United States tends to focus on rote facts and procedures rather than on helping students solve problems, build networks of knowledge, and consolidate that knowledge into larger and more useful conceptual systems. To change this, Romberg and Kaput (1999) suggest that mathematics instruction needs to provide students with activities that help them understand why certain techniques work, invite them to experiment with new techniques, and help them learn to question as well as justify their own (and others') assertions. Helping students learn how users of mathematics think through a problem, make decisions about what to quantify and how, and make predictions and judge their robustness becomes an instructional priority. From my perspective, this view of instruction calls for engaged mathematical thinking through envisionment building.

LEARNING MATHEMATICS BY
ENGAGING IN APPLIED ACTIVITIES

Based on their studies at the National Research Center in Mathematical Sciences Education, Carpenter and Lehrer (1999) suggest that mathematics learning occurs through real-world application rather than by first being taught the concept or process and then applying it. Students construct their own knowledge when they engage in mathematics activities that give them room to understand the nature of the problem and its possibilities. Through engaging in problem-solving activities that invite generative thinking, students come face-to-face with—and learn to better understand complexities embedded in—the concepts, as well as relationships among the concepts and processes, that they are learning. In this way, through successive acts of envisionment building, their depth of understanding grows over time. They become aware of critical relationships among mathematical concepts and processes, and are increasingly able to apply that knowledge in new mathematical situations, in a variety of contexts. Importantly, Romberg and Kaput (1999) say that students learn mathematical language use through their need to think through, reason, compute, and communicate as well as to abstract, generalize, and formalize constructs that are appropriate to their problem-solving activities.

The envisionment-building classroom provides the context for active problem-solving, in which mathematical concept building and language development occur. Here, students are presented with mathematical problems in activity form. Calling upon potentially related networks of knowledge that they already have, they are guided to think through a problem, consider possible procedures that might lead to a solution, look ahead and forecast where they are headed, and reflect back on the usefulness of the meaning-building paths they have taken.

Instead of focusing on whether an answer is simply right or wrong, the emphasis is on envisionment building, gaining insights into what, why, and how things went right or wrong and what can be done to reach solutions. All this takes place in a minds-on and interactive classroom where thinking is made visible to all through discussion, writing, and other forms of representation. The goal is to provide a supportive communicative context where students can confront their preconceptions as well as recognize and work beyond them by engaging in activities in which students think through and apply mathematics concepts. The features of instruction (see Chapter 4)—building envisionments, forging curricular connections, orchestrating substantive and sustained discussion, and offering enabling strategies—underlie the pedagogy of the envisionment-building classroom.

Engaging in mathematical problem-solving, having opportunities to discuss possible solutions, and comparing and contrasting seemingly viable approaches puts students in the role of mathematical thinkers. They can learn ways to identify and explain why some approaches to particular problem-solving situations don't work well and come to understand why others seem to work better. Through this kind of metacognitive activity, students become aware of networks of knowledge that may be helpful to them. At the same time, their teachers can become aware of the specific content or procedural information that needs to be taught.

All this happens within a problem-solving context where content and process are linked in action. Interactive envisionment-building classrooms, such as those discussed in this book, help students make sense of their mathematical experiences; through discussion they learn ways to reflect, clarify, and modify their thinking (Yackel & Cobb, 1996). Together, they develop knowledge. Discussion and argumentation about mathematical problems are central to learning mathematics (see, for example, Carpenter, Franke, & Levi, 2003; Schifter, 1996); as in other subjects, students need to learn the language and structure of mathematics—how to think about and with it and how to communicate about and with it.

Following is an example of a high school mathematics class. Although all the concepts I have discussed in Chapters 1–4 are occurring, in this and the following example I will highlight the envisionment-building stances the students enter as well as some features of minds-on instruction as the students attempt to understand and learn mathematics.

SUSTAINED DISCUSSION AND PROBLEM SOLVING FOR 12TH-GRADE STRUGGLING MATHEMATICIANS

Let us look at Jason Mutford's 12th-grade class. His students were taking his "decelerated" geometry course in preparation for the examination they needed to pass in order to graduate from high school with a regular diploma. All were struggling math students. Most of them were seniors, with a couple of juniors who were repeating that grade. All had "fallen out of their usual track" and were taking the one-semester geometry course for a full year as a way to get sufficient help to pass the state exam. The year had started with ten students in class, but three soon dropped out of school entirely. Of the remaining seven, three had taken and failed this course once before, while the remaining students had been recommended by their previous year's teachers. The majority of the coursework focused on the logic of geometry proofs.

Mr. Mutford had recently transformed his approach to teaching, with envisionment building as his goal and minds-on teaching as his instructional approach. When asked to describe this, he said,

> I began to realize that [before] I was not so much teaching my
> class on Euclidean geometry proofs as I was pulling it along like
> an ox shackled to a yoke. The students had obliged me, working
> haphazardly and dispassionately on homework assignments. The

class had to be reinvented completely. . . . I had an awakening where I realized I am the one at the board who's been talking, who needs to sit down and have them start talking about the math. I realized they were using the symbols as a crutch. They could move the symbols around and sometimes get it right, but they were still falling for misconceptions, pitfalls, traps. They really didn't have a depth to understanding the logic, which is weird because logic is something people use without realizing it, but when you bring it into a math class and put symbols on it, they regard it as something completely new.

Unlike so many of us who have epiphanies but don't pick up on them, Mr. Mutford followed through. He completely redesigned his approach and created an envisionment-building class.

Students as Problem-Solvers

To shift the focus from himself as teller to his students as problem-solvers, Mr. Mutford explained to his students that in the future, they would take turns at the board and become "scribes" while everyone else in class would be responsible for what the scribe put on the board; the group would do the thinking. This sort of group problem-solving would require a lot of discussion, thought, and checking, and everyone would need to be involved—all the time. With this beginning shift, he set his minds-on classroom in motion. The students understood that his focus would be on their own envisionment building, with substantive and sustained discussion and joint problem-solving as a means to do this.

In commenting on how this approach might work in a larger class, he said that at times he would break them into smaller groups and then bring them together. At other times, one group would have a spokesperson and scribe and the rest of the class would interact to move their work ahead. Yet other times, he would have the class watch one group work and the others react. At still other times, he would divide the class in two and have the groups work in tandem. The goal in each case would be to engage the students in discussion, to approach proofs as problems rather than as exercises, and to sharpen the students' mathematical literacy as they sharpened their ability to develop and reflect on their proofs.

Clearly, as a geometry class, the primary purpose of the activity was to develop proofs, and thus point-of-reference thinking, with the finished proof as the point toward which they were aiming, the goal. For students at every level of mathematics development, Mr. Mutford wanted to help them learn to listen to their own voices as well as to one another's, to question and build upon or disagree with what others said, but always to move the conversation and the conceptualization forward by explaining why they didn't agree or by making alternative suggestions. Throughout, the students learned to engage in mathematical thinking while also learning appropriate vocabulary and proof-writing strategies.

We can see this happening when his class works on parallelograms. Mr. Mutford starts the lesson by showing the students the diagram in Figure 7.1 and telling them specifically what two things they need to prove:

> Start as a whole group, and decide as a whole group if you're actu-
> ally going to do two separate proofs or go right through to prove
> both parallelograms. Everyone is responsible for their own partici-
> pation. . . . You have three givens and you have to prove two dif-
> ferent things [are parallelograms]: 1) the outside figure and 2) the
> center band. It's open notes, open discussion, open textbooks. You
> can use textbooks, the notes you took, each other.

Figure 7.1. The Parallelogram Problem

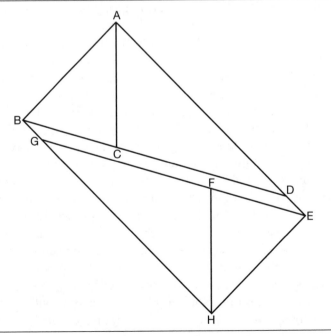

Students as Mathematics Thinkers

When questions arise about where to start, Mr. Mutford lets the students discuss and decide how they will begin to do the proofs. He wants them to think this through and learn to look ahead. In the next excerpt, you can see by Lilia's remark that they are used to engaging in substantive and sustained discussion with one another as she quickly poses a way to begin—in this case, which parallelogram to solve for first. Following her suggestion, her classmates work with one another, thinking aloud about what they have and what they might solve. Here, because they are in the first stance (Getting Started with the Material; see Chapter 2), they are trying to gather enough ideas to begin to form a thin envisionment—a place from which to start building. (Note that Jose is the scribe.)

> *Lilia*: [to her classmates] So, we'll do the outside one first, and get it out of the way, right?
> *Jose*: [thinking things through aloud] I don't know. It may be easier to do the inside thing first—do all the triangles. BGED and ABHE are parallelograms. If you prove all the triangles you still don't really have it. Wait, no. If you prove those inside 4 triangles, you win.
> *David*: Well, AC is the perpendicular bisector. Perpendicular is 90 degrees, isn't it?
> *Lilia*: Then it's a right angle, right?
> *Jose*: Perpendicular? Yeah, that's 90 degrees. . . .
> *Helen*: What if we prove HBA and AEH are obtuse?
> *Jose*: They're not obtuse at all.
> *Lilia*: What about ABE and HEG?
> *Helen*: So, AC is congruent to FH. . . .

After this brainstorming, the students work on the problem informally by themselves or quietly with someone sitting close by. Although they are at different levels of understanding, all the students are focusing on the proof and are searching for a way in. Then Greg wants the group to consider the givens as potential help. Although Mr. Mutford remains silent much of the time, giving the students opportunities to think aloud, he offers enabling strategies in ways to think—in the form of think abouts at points of need. You will see that David enters the fourth stance (Thinking Critically About the Material) because he becomes aware of what he needs to know and wants to fill in.

Greg: What are the givens?

Jose: [reading from board]

Segment BG is congruent to Segment DE.

Segment AC is congruent to Segment FH.

Segment BC is congruent to Segment FE.

Segment AC is perpendicular bisector of segment BD and the bisector of BAD.

Segment FH is perpendicular bisector of Segment EG and the bisector of EHG.

David: What's a bisector?

Mr. Mutford: [scribe points and teacher says] See, if it bisects an angle, if it also bisects a segment or if it only bisects a segment. You have 3 choices there. . . .

Later on, several students try to identify congruence. They know this is needed for their proof. Again, at point of need, Mr. Mutford steps in to offer a helpful enabling strategy about how to think about the problem, but not an answer. The students are in the second stance (Developing Understanding of the Material) as they are immersed in narrowing the possibilities and developing their proof. See how they work together to do this.

Helen: BG and DE are parallelograms.

Jose: BD and GE are congruent.

Greg: We haven't said they're congruent yet. It's the bisector in the middle.

Helen: What about BD and GE?

Jose: BD and GE are congruent. Right?

Mr. Mutford: Whoa, whoa, you don't know that yet. You haven't said they're congruent. You just know that they got bisected. Rethink #6.

Lilia: What about BC and CD and then GFE?

Mr. Mutford: It's not that easy. You just know that they got bisected. Rethink #6.

Mr. Mutford's suggestion is what Greg needs. He blurts out his ideas to his classmates, and they join in problem-solving. Learning to do proofs is at the center of their focus. See how, in the second stance (Developing Understanding of the Material), they are making more rapid progress.

Greg: I got this one now. . . . Use the addition postulate, 'cause the bisector is in the middle. BC add to CD. And EF add to FG. They are congruent. . . . Then BD is congruent to GE, so it makes the small parallelogram. . . . Add CB and CD and the bisector cuts them right in the middle. You get that BD is congruent to GE. . . .

Lilia: AH and HA are reflexive.

Greg: [excited and using his book as reference] Use the bisector to break them down to BC, CD, GF, and FE. [Reads definition of a parallelogram and paraphrases, "One pair of opposite sides are congruent and parallel, 2 pairs of opposite sides are congruent pairwise."] We have them. Definition of a parallelogram.

Jose: [Scribe writes the proof and reason on the board.]

Lilia: So now we need to break them down, right? We have to get those two separate bases, BD, CD. To get those 2 separate bases.

Helen: To prove the parallelogram. ABD and HGE. . . .

As this productive talk continues, Jose pulls aside and scans his text and notes. Watch how he opens a new line of thinking that the others then join. At one point, David enters the conversation from the fourth stance (Thinking Critically About the Material), judging what they have already figured out and pointing out what they need to rethink before moving on. Look at their progress afterward.

Helen to Jose: What are you doing? [He is busily writing on the board.]

Jose: It says [referring to book], this is perpendicular if there are right angles and we didn't mention them and it doesn't count unless we do. [He adds them to board.]

All: [Silence, thinking]

Jose: Now, since we have the parallelogram, we can subtract and partial it—subtract this from this together to make the huge parallelogram. Use the bisector to break them down to BC, CD, GF, and FE.

Greg: Yeah, break it back down and we have both bases of the triangle. Then add them back together, you have a hypotenuse and leg almost.

David: Yeah, and then prove that GF and FE are congruent.

Jose: Yeah, and then add them together to get that huge
    parallelogram. . . .
Helen: BC and CD are congruent to the bisector.
Jose: But all 4 need to be congruent.
David: We need to prove the triangles are the same.

Once again, Mr. Mutford intercedes and offers guidance on ways to think
and ways to do to approach the problem. See how quickly the students
pick up on what he says each time, and continue to build from there.

Mr. Mutford: There are 2 distinctly incorrect things in the proof
    [proof on the board], triangle things. . . .
Jose: If we're trying to de-prove those parts, if we break those
    stupid segments back down. . . . We once had them. We should
    break them back down. Or maybe we should have started with
    the big one, not the little one. . . .
Mary: The big triangle really bothers me.
Greg: [Goes to statement 6 on the board] That's how we did it.
Mr. Mutford: Those are weak, but not necessarily wrong. Get
    behind statement 6. You didn't have enough information then
    to justify statement 6. Instead of erasing it, go back to it and set
    it up properly.
Jose: So, 5½.
Mr. Mutford: There you go.
David: BC and CD are congruent.
Lilia: I was right about them last time. BC and CD, GF and FE are
    congruent, I said it. . . .
All: [Think and talk with one another; look at teacher]
Mr. Mutford: Are all 4 little segments congruent or are all 4 pairs
    congruent?
David: All 4 are congruent. Oh no!
Mr. Mutford: This technique will take you so far, but to get to all 4
    you need more. It'll work in the end. . . .
Mr. Mutford: [Students look to him.] I want you to figure it out.
    I want it to be part of your discovery process. If I tell you
    everything I'll be telling you a story, but I want you to be part
    of the story. . . .
Lilia: [Goes up to the board and points to explain to them why she
    thinks they are congruent.] [difficult to hear]

Greg: What will that give us that we don't already know?

Lilia: It'll move over to the parallelogram. The one in the middle. You need to prove that.

Jose: [Thinks aloud] The one side is congruent to the other side. BG, DE prove they are congruent. That definition of parallelogram, that'll prove the angles are the same.

Lilia: But there's more. [Points to segments]

Jose: [Looks at book for reference in response to her comments]

Lilia: [Makes additional explanations about angles and sides]

All: [Silence, thinking and reading book and notes; whispering about where to go next]

Jose: So, take this segment out to this segment and this one to this?

Lilia: Yes.

All: [Work silently or in pairs, searching for next steps]

As the class period is about to end, Mr. Mutford does not wrap up the class by telling the students how they should have completed their proofs. He wants them to continue to think and reason about their process as well as content. See what he says to help them continue.

Mr. Mutford: I want to wrap this thought up because we're running low on time. Don't freak out about not having a finished proof as far as your assessment is concerned. Your assessment is on your process, not on your product being a finished product.

Jose: But we can finish it?

Mr. Mutford: We can pick this back up tomorrow. The other thing is, there are still a couple of holes in your proof. The addition postulate he just put down is true, but I don't think you have all the statements you need before #14 to justify it. It's a matter of putting all the information in the right sequence. So at one point we're going to have to fix up the sequence. The concept is correct. The sequence needs fixing. Some of your statements are out of order. I'll put all this on an overhead so tomorrow we can look at it and work. Sound like a plan?

Students: Yes. Good. Okay.

Figure 7.2 shows the work the scribe had written on the board (the final work at the end of the period, after many changes and erasures).

Figure 7.2. The Proof at the End of the First Day

Statement	Reasons
1. $\overline{DE} \cong \overline{DG}$	given
2. $\overline{AC}$ is perpendicular bisector of $\angle BAD$	given
3. $\overline{FH}$ is perp. bisector of $\angle EHG$	given
4. $\overline{AC} \cong \overline{AC}$	reflexive property
5. $\overline{FH} \cong \overline{FH}$	same as 4
6. $\overline{BD} \cong \overline{GH}$	addition post state
7. $\angle F$ BDEG	def. of parallelogram
8. $\angle BCA$ & $\angle DCA$ are rt. Angles	def of perpendicular (2)
9. $\angle GFH$ & $\angle BFH$ are rt angles	def of perpendicular (3)
10. $\overline{BC} \cong \overline{CP}$	def of bisector
11. $\overline{GF} \cong \overline{FE}$	def of bisector, same as 11
12. $\triangle ABC = \triangle ABD$	parallel (4, 8, 10)
13. $\triangle HGF = \triangle HFE$	parallel (5, 9, 11)
14. $\overline{BH} \cong \overline{AE}$	addition positive

Reflecting on the Approach

This was a minds-on activity. It invited all the students to become engaged in the material, whatever their level of geometry knowledge, and left room for their envisionments to build. In addition to moving toward developing the proof, they gained important experiences in ways to understand what proofs are as well as ways to go about solving for them. Mr. Mutford provided effective instruction in response to what the students were thinking and doing. From his point-of-need guidance, they were able to gain a better understanding of what to think about, how to think, and what to do.

Throughout the class session, the students were fully engaged, and their thinking was visible. They flexibly engaged in both horizons-of-possibilities and point-of-reference thinking based on what they thought they knew or were after. They also entered the first, second, and fourth stances (Getting Started with the Material, Developing Understanding of the Material, and Thinking Critically About the Material), drawing on different approaches to allow their envisionments to develop. While they worked out geometry proofs, they learned to use mathematically appropriate processes, symbols, language, and thinking.

Mr. Mutford encouraged them to use what they knew and to venture into making sense of the new. They used the critical-thinking strategies listed in Chapter 4 as a matter of course, in helping them make sense of the problem, reflect on their preconceptions as well as their ideas and evidence, and question their assumptions and look for alternative paths that might be more efficacious. Because of this, they could agree, disagree, and build upon what others had said. They worked together, but took individual responsibility for understanding and working toward offering proofs and reasons. Although all students in this class were struggling geometry learners, they were at different levels of mathematical development. Yet each was offering, and each was learning. The nature of the activity provided opportunities for each of them to use logic in creating geometry proofs, Mr. Mutford's goal for the class.

Here is what one student said about the class at the end of the term: "I liked the class because I finally got it." Another said, "I was sorry this class was first period. This way I was stuck having to be in classes after where I couldn't think or understand as much." Mr. Mutford was pleased because "one of my catchphrases is to have my students risk success. Instead of points off, they can earn it all. Now they can do proofs on their own."

AN 8TH-GRADE CLASS DEVELOPING
MATH CONCEPTS THROUGH PROBLEM-BASED ACTIVITIES

Now let us look at Randall Roeser's envisionment-building math class. It is a mainstreamed 8th-grade class, with students at a range of ability levels. Three students have been identified as having special needs. Although the content is, of course, different from Mr. Mutford's, there are similarities in the structure of the activity; in the ways in which the students think, participate, and learn; and in the kinds of assistance that Mr. Roeser gives.

Writing and Discussion in a Structured Problem-Solving Activity

During a unit on angles, Mr. Roeser begins a lesson by asking his students to look at their notes and some diagrams on his interactive SMART Board, and to come up with definitions of adjacent, complementary, and supplementary angles. He wants them to move through the first stance (Getting Started with the Material), gathering enough ideas to be ready to make curricular connections and form an envisionment more easily in the next lesson. The students work in groups of four to develop their definitions. After each group presents and the others question them and provide feedback, Mr. Roeser says,

> *Mr. Roeser*: I'm thinking of two angles. The two angles are supplementary. What else would you need to know to tell me the measures of both angles? [Pause—no responses] For example, suppose one angle is 125 degrees, what is the other?
> *Students*: 55 degrees.
> *Mr. Roeser*: So, you only need to know one to get both. Why?
> *Students*: They both add up to 180 degrees.
> *Mr. Roeser*: Yes, and this is an introduction to what we'll be doing today. You don't always need to know the size of both angles.

On the SMART Board, he shows the goal of the lesson: "I can find the measures of angles formed by 2 intersecting lines."

> *Mr. Roeser*: Show me parallel lines with your fingers. What are the intersecting lines?
> *Students*: [Confused] None. There aren't any.
> *Mr. Roeser*: What are intersecting lines?
> *Students*: [No responses]
> *Mr. Roeser*: Show me with your fingers. [They show crossed fingers.] Now say it.
> *Michael*: Two lines that meet at a point.
> *Mr. Roeser*: Draw intersecting lines on your page. [He does this on the SmartBoard at the same time; see Figure 7.3.]
> *Mr. Roeser*: When you join 2 lines, how many angles are there?
> *Students*: Four.

Mr. Roeser writes numerals 1, 2, 3, and 4 within the angles and then says:

Figure 7.3. The Intersecting Lines Problem

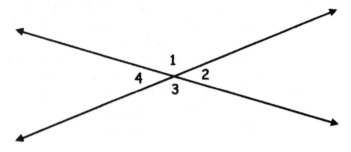

Intersecting lines cross at a single point and form four angles.

So, this is your problem for today. It's the intersecting lines problem. [Shows it on overhead.] Two lines intersect to form four angles. What is the least number of angles you would have to measure with a protractor in order to know the measurement of all four angles?

Until now, the exchanges have been in the form of a review, but this concept is entirely new. To help his students make a connection, Mr. Roeser scaffolds the students in ways to think about and do the work:

This is like the question I just asked before: How many angles would you need to know to figure out the other angles (1, 2, 3, and 4)? You can use protractors or just think it out in your minds. Work in groups and write your answer in a paragraph. Begin it with, "In order to find the size of the angles of 2 intersecting lines you need to know _____. This is because _____."

Once again, the students meet in groups to brainstorm, share ideas, and discuss. They are working in the second stance (Developing Understanding of the Material) as they try to solve the problem, with the number of angles of intersecting lines they need to know to determine the others, as their point of reference. In one group, a student begins by saying, "You will have to know 2 angles to tell them all, because then you could subtract from 180 degrees." A special education student begins to measure the angles with a protractor, planning to get all the angles and work backward. While they are reasoning through the problem and proposing solutions, Mr. Roeser moves from group to group, providing additional enabling strategies at point of need. Some students argue that you need to know two angles, some one, but there is no unanimous agreement in any group. Mr. Roeser's questions prod them to think in new directions. At the end of class, with them still trying to solve the problem, he says, "Tomorrow we will discuss the findings of your group."

In recounting the lessons that followed, Mr. Roeser writes:

> The lesson was concluded over the next 2 days. The first of those days . . . I gave the students the final 10 minutes . . . to continue discussing, in their groups, the intersecting lines problem that I had posed the previous day. . . .
>
> The following day . . . I got back to the intersecting lines problem. I restated the lesson goal and called on three groups to present their conclusions. I selected the groups and the order of presentation strategically, based on my observations of the group work over the previous two days. I wanted students to hear conflicting conclusions and different methods for arriving at those conclusions.
>
> Note that although each group reported separately, every student in the class had a role in identifying and commenting on the conflicting answers and explanations.
>
> One of the selected groups decided that you needed to know the measures of two different angles. They had measured all four angles and found that each pair of nonadjacent angles had the same measure. Since there were two pairs of nonadjacent angles, they concluded that you needed to measure one angle in each pair.
>
> The second group had also measured all four angles but came to a different conclusion. They noted that pairs of adjacent angles are supplementary. They reasoned that, knowing the measure of just one angle, you could subtract that measure from $180°$ to get the measure of an adjacent angle. Like the first group, their measurements had led to the observation that nonadjacent angles are equal. So, once they had the measures of the two adjacent supplementary angles, they knew the measures of all four angles. The second group thus concluded that you need to measure only one angle in order to know all four.

The third group also concluded that just one angle needed to be measured, but used a different approach. They didn't measure any angles. Rather, they used their knowledge of supplementary angles to reason as follows: If you were to measure one angle, both of the angles that are adjacent to that angle would be supplements of the measured angle. By subtracting the measured angle from 180° you know the measure of those two adjacent angles. That leaves just one unknown angle, but it is adjacent and supplementary to two angles, whose measures have been figured out and are the same. The difference between 180° and the measure of one of those adjacent angles yields the measure of the fourth angle.

Note the progression of thinking from one group to the next. The first group reasoned from a limited number of examples that nonadjacent angles are equal. But they stopped there and concluded that two angles must be measured. Arguing from cases is a weaker form of proof in mathematics but it set the stage for the other approaches.

The second group also took an inductive approach but went a step further by connecting the concept of supplementary angles to reduce the number of required measurements to one.

The third group eschewed induction and made, in effect, a deductive proof built on their knowledge of adjacent supplementary angles. In the process, they discovered what others had observed from their measurements—namely, that nonadjacent angles formed by two intersecting lines are equal. The power of their deductive approach was that they could explain why the nonadjacent angles are equal. This is the beginning of the formal reasoning that is the foundation of high school geometry.

Because he wanted all students to continue to build envisionments, during each presentation Mr. Roeser invited the class to question, agree, disagree, or add to what the presenting group had said. It was an open and rich discussion.

The lessons presented so far led directly to the concept of vertical angles, the nonadjacent angles formed when two lines intersect. As Mr. Roeser explained, "As the first two groups conjectured and the third group proved beyond doubt, vertical angles are always equal. We took time at that point for students to make an entry for vertical angles in the vocabulary section of their notebook."

The sequence continued with some applications on other sets of intersecting lines, and finally a task in which the students were given the measure of one angle and asked to state the measures of the other three. Again, in Mr. Roeser's words, "This stark exercise was intended to crystallize in students' minds the idea that, when two (nonperpendicular) lines intersect, you get four angles but just two different angle measures, and those two angle measures add to 180°."

The lessons on angles concluded with a reflective writing exercise designed to help students integrate their investigations into intersecting lines, and to show the kinds of reasoning, inductive or deductive, they had used to solve their problem. As in their discussions, mathematical reasoning and mathematical language were necessary to fulfill the writing assignment—not just the vocabulary, but ways to express themselves in mathematical terms and form. After instructions about layout and presentation, including use of a self-assessment rubric (see Figure 7.4), the task had two parts:

Mathematical Reflections

Big Idea: Angles formed by intersecting lines

a. Two lines intersect to form angles. What is the fewest number of angles that you would need to measure with a protractor in order to know the measures of all four angles? Support your answer with a detailed explanation.
b. Two lines intersect to form four angles. The measure of one angle is x degrees. How would you represent the measures of the other three angles in terms of x? Explain your thinking.

Once again, mathematical reasoning and language are needed to fulfill the assignment.

Here are two examples of student responses to part A. Mr. Roeser highlighted the italicized words to emphasize proper use of technical vocabulary, crossed out unnecessary words, and added the bracketed comments to the student work, all reinforcing the proper expression of mathematical concepts.

a.   In order to find the measures of all four angles you would only need to measure one [correct!] angle with a *protractor*. Let's

Figure 7.4. Rubric for Assessment and Self-Reflection

	Level 1	Level 2	Level 3	Rater's Marks
Task Understanding	Demonstrates *little* to *no* understanding of the task	Demonstrates *partial* understanding of the task	Demonstrates *thorough* understanding of the task	Comment if you did not follow directions, did not complete the task, or misunderstood the task.
Conceptual Understanding	Demonstrates *little* or *no* understanding of the key concepts or "big ideas" in the task.	Demonstrates *partial* understanding of the key concepts or "big ideas" in the task.	Demonstrates *thorough* understanding of the key concepts or "big ideas" in the task.	Notation in margin: C Example of Level 2 understanding C+ Example of Level 3 understanding
Level of Thinking	Thinking limited to knowledge and comprehension • facts • descriptions	Demonstrates analytical thinking • explains • justifies • connects • classifies • compares and contrasts • illustrates • prioritizes • breaks down	Demonstrates synthetic or evaluative thinking. • generalizes • predicts • conjectures • critiques • judges • draws conclusions • recommends	Highlighted text: Yellow Example of Level 2 thinking Pink Example of Level 3 thinking
Evidence	Presents *little* or *no* evidence (facts, details) to support argument.	Presents *some* evidence to support argument.	Presents *extensive* evidence to support argument.	Checkmark on each piece of evidence
Vocabulary	Uses *little* or *no* vocabulary of discipline accurately.	Uses *some* vocabulary of discipline accurately.	Uses *extensive* vocabulary of discipline accurately.	Box or loop around correct vocabulary usage. Parentheses around incorrect vocabulary usage
Mechanics	*Many* errors in grammar, capitalization, spelling, and punctuation.	*Some* errors in grammar, capitalization, spelling, and punctuation.	*Few or no* errors in grammar, capitalization, spelling, and punctuation.	See English editing marks

call the angle we already know angle J. The measure of the angle *vertical* to angle J is equal to angle J because vertical angles are equal. So now we know half of the angles we need to know. Angle J is *adjacent* to another angle, the angle will be called O. Angle J and angle O are *supplementary* angles (two angles when adjacent form a 180-degree angle). This means that angle O is 180 – the measure of angle J. Since we know that vertical angles are equal, the measure of angle vertical to angle O is equal to angle O.

a.   The fewest number of angles you would need is one [correct!] because for two *intersecting* lines to form four *angles* the [adjacent] angles would have to be *supplementary* (equals 180 degrees). Say that one angle equaled 76 degrees. The angle *vertical* of the 76 degree angle would have the same angle measure becuse it is straight across, or, *vertical*. To find the other two [adjacent] angles you would only have to subtract 76 degrees from 180 because as mentioned earlier [adjacent] angle[s] [are] is supplementary. 180 – 76 = 104 so the other two angles that are *vertical* to each other would be 104 degrees.

Throughout the year, Mr. Roeser encouraged his students to extend their envisionments by making connections between the mathematical principles and ways of thinking they were learning in class and their applications to issues or situations that appear in everyday life. He felt these connections would lead to deeper understandings as well as better applications of the concepts.

Working with Ratios

During another part of his work with this class, Mr. Roeser wanted his students to develop a deeper understanding of ratios, what they mean, and how they work. Embedded in his longer unit on ratios, he asked his students to identify a topic that interested them and had some underlying data that were available to be compared. One example he offered was to choose a particular animal and the ratio of their survival to the food they eat. Although it was primarily a point-of-reference activity, he gave his students much leeway in deciding what to report about and how to present it. Therefore, sometimes students engaged in horizons of possibilities to choose the topics and to explore the ways in which they might proceed. After researching their topic online and elsewhere, the students developed PowerPoint presentations to use in oral reports to their class and the school principal.

Figure 7.5 shows the central calculations and conclusions from two slides from one group's presentation on the survival of pandas. The students went on to conclude that if the panda population continued to expand as it had in the past 30 years, "the pandas will come out of extinction ☺."

Figure 7.5 PowerPoint Slides Applying Ratios in the Real World

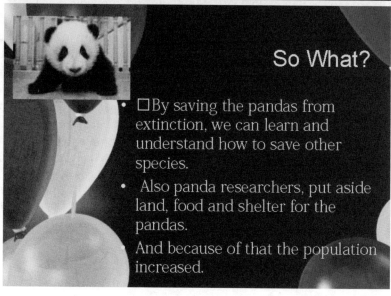

Here, too, Mr. Roeser offers his students enabling strategies, this time in the form of a percentage of change rubric (see Figure 7.6). Before the students make their presentations, they are given the rubric to use as a guide as they are developing their presentations, and later to give evaluative feedback to their classmates. Mr. Roeser considers mathematical communication to be an essential component of mathematical concept development as well as mathematical literacy. Thus, he considers electronic and graphic as well as oral presentations as important as written work as evidence of student learning.

SUMMING UP

Envisionment-building classrooms such as Mr. Mutford's and Mr. Roeser's are the kinds of minds-on environments that invite all students into disciplinary activity and provide ongoing opportunities for them to learn. Students are invited to think mathematically and use mathematical language. In these classes, students begin by thinking of their own envisionments, but soon go beyond. They learn from the range of materials at their disposal and from one another as well as from their teachers. But they are challenged to become increasingly familiar with mathematical language, thinking, and problem-solving. Students are involved in working through and coming to understand the kinds of conceptual and procedural issues that are at the heart of mathematical thinking and knowing.

The class work is planned around activities that bring students into direct conceptual confrontation with the data they must learn to manipulate. The teachers provide students with strategies for ways to think about the content as well as ways to understand the assignment, to plan and carry out the assignment, and to reflect on and evaluate how well they have done. In this environment, students don't merely learn to compute right answers but to reason mathematically. They use vocabulary, organize their ideas, and present evidence in a manner that is appropriate for mathematics, and interact about mathematical concepts in ways that show they understand. As they become more mathematically literate, they continue to build the deeper knowledge that will be useful within and beyond the school doors, throughout their lives.

Figure 7.6. Rubric for Percentage of Change Activity

	1	2	3	4	Points
Organization	Audience cannot understand presentation because there is no sequence of information.	Audience has difficulty following presentation because students jump around.	Students present information in logical sequence that audience can follow.	Students present information in logical, interesting sequence that audience can follow.	____
Content Knowledge	Students do not demonstrate knowledge of percentage of change; students cannot answer questions about subject.	Students have limited knowledge of percentage of change and are able to answer only rudimentary questions.	Students demonstrate knowledge of percentage of change but make minor errors or fail to elaborate.	Students demonstrate full knowledge of percentage of change with explanations and elaboration.	____
Visuals	Students use no visuals.	Students occasionally use visuals that rarely support text and presentation.	Students use visuals that relate to text and presentation.	Students use visuals to reinforce screen text and presentation.	____
Elements	Presentation includes fewer than 4 of the required elements.	Presentation includes at least 4 of the required elements.	Presentation includes 6 of the required elements.	Presentation includes all 7 required elements.	____
Delivery	Students make little or no eye contact. Students mumble, pronounce terms incorrectly, and speak too quietly for people in the back of class to hear.	Students make limited eye contact with audience. Students incorrectly pronounce terms. Audience members have difficulty hearing presentation.	Students make some eye contact with audience. Students use clear voices and pronounce most terms correctly.	Students make frequent eye contact with audience. Students use clear voices and pronounce terms correctly.	____
				Subtotal (20 pts. max.) →	____

CHAPTER 8

Envisionment Building
in English

The goal of present-day English education, by and large, is to develop a literate and cultured populace that has a deep knowledge of literary traditions as well as the ability to read with ease, write fluently, think deeply, and communicate effectively. (See, for example, the NCTE/IRA Standards for the English Language Arts, 2009.) Therefore, English coursework focuses on reading, writing, and literature as well as on oral language and information/communication technology—on the uses and production of language as well as on the knowledge and experiences we convey through language. Literature is at the heart of what is to be learned, while reading, writing, and oral language are modes through which we gain and convey our thoughts and understandings.

THINKING WITH AND THROUGH LANGUAGE

Many aspects of our experience affect how we think both with and through language. Of course, the content and the medium in which it is presented affect how we think, but so do the social, cultural, and textual conventions as well as life experiences that are embedded in the messages. These "hidden" features can make a significant difference in what we understand and how we respond to it. One responsibility of the English teacher is to help students gain sufficient control of language and sufficient familiarity with a range of language uses (including textual and cultural variations) to enable them to recognize these "hidden" messages, to create thoughtful envisionments with them and develop thoughtful responses to them.

Students learn that there is no one "correct" interpretation of literary works. Rather, interpretations are a function of the reader's life and literary experiences as well as cultural history. Although students also need to learn "received interpretations," their own may differ; good interpretations are ones that can be defended well. Since language is the primary medium for teaching, growth, and change, students also need to learn ways to build and communicate knowledge effectively using a range of sources and in a range of presentational forms (e.g., Alverman & Hagood, 2000; Langer, 1986a, 1987; Lee, 2007; New London Group, 1987).

COGNITIVE AND LINGUISTIC ASPECTS OF ENGLISH LEARNING

Effective learners are problem-solvers and decision-makers. Achieving this requires us to focus on the cognitive and linguistic processes involved in learning and teaching (see, for example, Alverman et al., 1996; Chang-Wells & Wells, 1992; Close, Hull, & Langer, 2005; Gambrell & Almasi, 1996; Guthrie & Wigfield, 2000; Lee, 2007; Pressley, Allington, Wharton-McDonald, Block, & Morrow, 2001). From the perspective of envisioning knowledge, students must be able to interpret, analyze, evaluate, and critique information, as they conduct research by raising questions, posing problems, and generating ideas. They are expected to be active and minds-on students who engage in the kinds of knowledge-building activities discussed in Chapter 4.

To help their envisionments grow, students must also be able to explore horizons of possibilities. As I discuss in the second edition of *Envisioning Literature*, the horizons-of-possibilities orientation dominates when the primary purpose is to step into the text and engage in a literary experience (Langer, 2010; Rosenblatt, 1938/1978) when readers step into unforeseen paths or create imaginary worlds. However, horizons of possibilities is not necessarily the primary orientation all of the time. Instead, point of reference is the primary purpose in reading literature when the main goal is to learn more about the content, text, or author. In these cases, the primary mind-set is to develop understanding of a particular point (e.g., to do a new historical reading); thus, the primary orientation would be point of reference. Each orientation adds breadth of understanding; they work together to enrich understanding. One goal of the envisionment-building English language arts class is to help students learn to call on both orientations, each when appropriate for their purpose, as they build rich envisionments of the texts. In this chapter, we will focus on the kinds of experiences that occur during this process, whichever is the primary orientation.

The English classroom is the major forum in which students learn about language, and also learn through using language, to understand, to think critically about, and to gain knowledge from works representing a wide range of genres. Thus, the critical-thinking strategies discussed in Chapter 4 play out as students raise questions, refine understandings, make interpretations, develop summaries, take positions and question assumptions, and posit explanations and defenses.

Research and scholarship in English for at least the last 25 years have indicated that effective thinking and learning are situated in students' language use, including experiences in writing, discussion, and interactive media. James Britton strongly influenced this movement in the field of English. (See, for instance, Britton, 1970.) Much work on classroom interactions followed (e.g., Applebee, Langer, Nystrand, & Gamoran, 2003; Chang-Wells & Wells, 1992; Gutierriez, 1993; Nystrand, 1997).

As early as 1969, James Britton's studies demonstrated that students not only write to learn but also speak to learn, and they do this by participating in substantive exchanges with one another as well as with their teachers. Learning emerges from the interplay of voices (Bakhtin, 1981, 1986). We are stimulated to learn and think about what others say, and even when we do not agree with their ideas, we reflect on our own and can sharpen our thinking. If someone's point is well defended, we have the option to keep it available in memory as a viable interpretation, even when it is different from ours.

We also learn through the act of writing. Langer and Applebee's studies (1987) remind us that the types of writing students are asked to do make a difference in what they will learn. Writing that requires students to replicate the information in the text leads to limited learning of that particular information, and is not remembered long. More extensive assignments that require students to elaborate and reformulate lead to deeper and more conceptually rich learning that is remembered longer. Overall, discussion, writing, and the manipulation of content and ideas with technology (e.g., Gee, 2007; Scardamalia, 2006; Zhang, 2009) play critical roles in student learning. They work best when embedded in activities where students' envisionments have room to develop and that make connections between the content at the moment and related big ideas within the field or the world (Applebee, 1996).

Because the content of English is so close to human experience, who the students are and the societal and cultural experiences they have had are of great concern (e.g., Lee, 2007; Willinsky, 1990). Instruction must assume that students already have some knowledge that they can connect to their new learnings, and activities must involve students in using their knowledge (of content and language) as they learn to expand both their linguistic and conceptual repertoires.

Because high literacy, the goal of English education, is by definition anchored in the technologies of the larger culture of the times, students must be able to learn from as well as communicate through the technologies that are found in their larger environments. However, for learning to occur, these experiences must be "minds-on," with students thoughtfully engaged with the content at hand (e.g., Alverman & Hagood, 2000; Flood, Heath, & Lapp, 1997; Gee, 2007; Rhodes & Robnolt, 2009).

Taking these issues into account, English teachers in an envisionment-building classroom elicit, value, and use the envisionments that students bring to school with them, and provide extensive opportunities for these to develop and grow. They plan activities that engage students in substantive language use, including discussion, writing, and reading (with print and technology) around critical topics and issues. When the activities engage students in examining and coming to understand important ideas and issues related to the topics under study, they will practice and learn the critical information, skills, and thinking strategies that are necessary for gaining knowledge and attaining high literacy.

HOW A 9TH-GRADE ENGLISH CLASS EXPLORES VOCABULARY AND CONTENT

Let us look at Ella Rosales's* 9th-grade English class. Her students have finished reading the short story "The Invalid's Tale" by Mark Twain. You will see that her students are used to interacting with one another in extended conversation. Although they frequently do this about the content of the piece and its meaning, here they are focusing on vocabulary, on the word *invalid* that is in the title. They also use their quest for word meaning as a way back into the text. See how, in this envisionment-building classroom, they work together to solve their problems.

> *Ms. Rosales*: All right. Now that you finished the story . . . we read the whole thing. Do you have any questions?

Andres: Why is it called the Invalid Story?

Ms. Rosales: That's a good question. [Looking at class] Why is it called the Invalid's Story?

At first, Ms. Rosales assumes that the students will use their discussion of the title as a way into discussing the piece and their interpretations of it, but Tanya's question and its resonance with the other students moves them to take a point-of-reference orientation that Ms. Rosales supports.

Tanya: What does *invalid* mean?

Ms. Rosales: That's another good question. Let's start with Tanya's. Let's see what we can come up with as a class and then we'll see what . . . [is] found in the dictionary. Randy . . .

Randy: I think it means the opposite of *valid*.

Ms. Rosales: The opposite of *valid*? I got you. Somebody give us another answer.

Anna: I'm going with go with what Randy said, that it's the opposite of something. Because like he thought the cheese was a dead body or something. . . .

Jack: Well, yesterday, he thought it was invalid, and it kind of goes along with what Anna said about the opposite of something. . . .

Ms. Rosales: Okay.

Jack: Valid is the opposite of invalid. . . . Invalid is like the wrong access code or something like that. And he had the wrong casket.

Exploring Word Meaning

As they discuss the word meaning, you will see that the students try to anchor their meanings to related aspects of the text, as Jack does. But they also look elsewhere for meaning, as Philip does.

Philip: I said like in the movies when they say put the password in and when they put it in, it says "invalid."

Ms. Rosales: Invalid. But remember we said it's not the invalid story, it's the invalid story.

Jack: Yeah, I know, but still.

Jing: Isn't *invalid* spelled the same way?

Ms. Rosales: It is spelled the same way, but we don't say it the same way.
(Lots of voices) . . .

At this point, the students become curious about language usage and multiple meanings for the same word.

Randy: Haley had a question. She said, "How, if it's spelled the same way, do you know which one it is?"
Ms. Rosales: That's a good question, how it's used in the sentence. But once you read the story, and you know what both definitions mean, then you have to ask yourself, "Which definition of this word fits the story?"
Greg: (Reading from dictionary) One incapacitated by chronic illness or injury. Ouch!

Based on their teacher's comment, the dictionary definition, and their own curiosity, the students return to the story to confront its contextualized meaning, with their teacher's help.

Ms. Rosales: So, if you're incapacitated by chronic illness or injury it means for some reason . . . what?
Randy: He's dead. . . .
Ms. Rosales: Who's the invalid here?
(Lots of voices)
Philip: The narrator. . . .
Ms. Rosales: [After some discussion] So, Randy, are you saying that the man who was killed was the invalid?
Randy: Yeah.
Ms. Rosales: So, some people—or at least Randy thinks that—some other people think the narrator was the invalid. What do you think? And tell us why.

At this point, Ms. Rosales provides a suggestion about ways to think about the question, meant to invite the students to take a closer look at the text, giving them direction as to what to think about.

Greg: Well, because it's his story, that's why they call it the invalid's story, and he's the main character of the story.

Ms. Rosales: And he's . . . ?

Students: The narrator.

Other Students: The invalid. . . .

Jacob: If I read it and didn't know if it was invalid or in-valid, I'd read it as in-valid.

Ms. Rosales: Jacob, why are you saying that?

Jacob: Because he's wrong. The guy's got the wrong box. It's in-valid. That's not right.

Randy: Maybe his friend is not really dead. Maybe his friend took a box and put the guns and limburger cheese in it.

Ms. Rosales: Well, how did the limburger cheese get there?

Randy: The little dude put some . . . didn't he have a hammer and some nails?

Exploring the Text

Next, you will see how Ms. Rosales offers another scaffold for ways to think, by pointing the students toward what to think about.

Ms. Rosales: Let's make sure everyone understands what's happening in the story. Look back at the first page. You should find the part about the limburger cheese, because there's a little footnote, a 1. So, find the 1 and then see if you can figure out what's going on. So, who put the limburger cheese there? . . .

Students: A stranger.

Ms. Rosales: Somebody walked in and put the cheese in a box . . . ? Jacob?

Jacob: The answer to Tanya's question after all that time, is that he said that when he went back to . . . and saw that person pointing at the box, he saw that his box was still there. He saw that somebody had moved his box and put another box there. And then when he looked at it he went back to wherever his box was and then he thought that his was still there. So that's when he brought it on board with him. . . .

Tanya: But he still should have looked.

Jacob: There would have been no story then. . . .

The discussion continues and the students now use both definitions with ease, understanding the dual meanings of the word *invalid* and the ways it could apply to the story. They have also learned the concept of heteronyms and have become alert to the possibilities that one spelling of a word might have more than one pronunciation as well as more than one meaning. In addition, when they think there may be a poor fit between the meaning of a word they know and the word they are reading, they know to consider whether it might be a heteronym (or homonym). When this happens, they also know to use the dictionary, and also to return to the story to figure out which meaning makes the best sense within the piece.

What is also interesting in this lesson is that the students were able to use the initial question about the meaning of a key word in the title as a way to revisit and rethink the entire story (not shown in this excerpted transcript) as well as a way to understand the word—one whose dual meanings they continued to use and refine, and will continue to refine as they see it used in the future.

During this lesson, the students primarily took a point-of-reference orientation toward word meaning, in response to Andres's question, "Why is it called the Invalid Story?" They knew they were after the meaning of *invalid* and worked on that problem until it was solved. But they soon move back into a horizon-of-possibilities orientation, where their focus is on understanding the story, using this understanding to identify the *invalid* referent, then moving from this awareness toward deeper understanding and interpretation.

MAKING LITERARY COMPARISONS IN 12TH-GRADE ENGLISH

Now let us look at Denise Wright's 12th-grade Honors English course titled "Introduction to Reading Literature." It is a "University at the High School" course that offers college as well as high school credit. Note the ways in which she uses envisionment-building approaches to help her students make comparisons in increasingly sophisticated ways. Her course description reads:

> This course will allow students the opportunity to learn the characteristics of a multitude of literary genres. Each genre will be addressed through representative authors for each. Students will apply standard techniques of literary analysis. Major emphasis is placed on improving the students' writing and discussion skills. Group projects and oral interpretation of works provide variety

within the curriculum. The expected outcomes are: Students will be able to (1) write using college-level thinking and style, (2) discuss material on a college level; (3) interpret, analyze, [and compare] all forms of literature, and (4) apply personal introspection to all forms of literature.

Comparing Poetic Styles

Ms. Wright begins a unit on Transcendentalism by having her students read and analyze poems by Ellery Channing and Henry David Thoreau. She tells them, "Keep your journal next to you. When you read these poems, do journal jots telling what your first impressions are." She does this as a way to help them focus on the philosophical as well as literary features that mark Transcendentalism writing. After discussion, she asks them to read works by Louisa May Alcott and compare them to Channing's poems, noting the similarities and differences. She reminds them that they need to focus on what the author is saying and how. Here the students are comparing the use of typical Transcendentalism content as well as the writers' techniques. The students begin by listing their reactions:

All about plants and flowers
Busy chanting stuff
Very hippie-like
Lot about nature
What about her life? . . .

Based on their comments, Ms. Wright thinks that although they will do research about the authors' lives and styles in the future, it would be helpful for them to be introduced to the authors as a way into making comparisons. The class continues:

Ms. Wright: I'll tell you a little about these authors so you'll be able to understand them better. Louisa May Alcott was born in 1832, and was a neighbor of Emerson. She was a tomboy with a love of nature. She wrote 30 books, from poetry to short stories. She was even a nurse during the Civil War. As you know, she wrote *Little Women.* Her poetry was overshadowed by her fiction. Look her up on the web like you did the others. You'll need it for when we go to Walden Pond next Tuesday.

Gladys: Why did she write *Little Men*?

Ms. Wright: Her sister had two children and needed money. She signed over the rights to her sister to let her sister have an income. . . . You wrote in your journal jots, as I did, that she wrote about everyday people. Now what do you know about Ellery Channing?

Greg: He was born in Boston.

Ms. Wright: Not too far from Walden Pond. Anything else?

Rick: Nothing.

Ms. Wright: Look him up on the web, too. He was born in 1880 and was brilliant, but different. His wife brought him into Transcendentalism. He and Thoreau were best buddies, and he was Thoreau's first biographer. Edgar Allan Poe, who lived around the same time, said his work was full of mistakes. He sticks heavily with nature, with the idea that nature helps us understand the universe. But his writing style, as you all said, was obscure. Now, take your chairs, and bring your poems, and move into a circle. Let's talk about both sets of poems. Let's start with Channing. Remember, when you compare, always focus on what the author is saying and how. Elements and form are always used as part of everyday discussion in literature.

Carol: It's hard, but about nature.

Frank: It's too long. Blah, blah, then nature. It could stop here. I like some but not all.

Paula: He says too much in each line. That makes it hard to follow. . . .

They analyze and discuss Channing's poems further and focus on the images or emotions he was describing, and then turn to Alcott.

Ms. Wright: Now, let's get to Louisa May Alcott.

Gladys: You could identify with something you had seen.

Walter: She's more down to earth.

Carol: Her language is simpler. . . .

Ms. Wright: Now, away from content, how did they handle the form and structure?

Frank: More patterns—stanzas.

Al: She sometimes turns story to rhyme. . . .

Ms. Wright: From what I'm hearing, you think there's more
    structure in Alcott. There is some structure in Channing, too.
Rick: But it's not where we're used to it.
Ms. Wright: Look back at his poems and see what you can find.
    . . . Now go back to your seats. We're going to do something
    with these individuals. Work in groups for 5 minutes to figure
    out what makes these writers different. We've talked about.
    . . . Now record it using a big T-chart in your groups. The
    categories are: [She writes on the board.]
    SOUND   FORM   USE OF ELEMENTS   EMOTIONS
Students: [Talking in groups] Channing, lots of emotions; Alcott,
    lots of sounds and emotions. . . .
Ms. Wright: [After 5 minutes] Which one is the biggest list you
    made?
Students: Emotions.

Ms. Wright then uses their response to lead to a major feature in Transcendental writing, the intensity of emotion:

Yes, in Transcendentalism it boils down to emotion. Channing's
writing is more difficult to understand at first, but his emotions
are behind it. Channing focuses on the intensity of nature, and as
you said, Alcott focuses on the intensity of family relations.

Later:

Tuesday, we'll go to Concord House to see Emerson's study and
Thoreau's desk, the Old Manse where Emerson lived and many of
the Transcendentalists wrote, and to Orchard House where Louisa
May Alcott grew up. Then we'll go to Walden Pond at Author's
Ridge and then to Sleepy Hollow Cemetery. You'll have a chance
to see where they lived and influenced one another. Remember to
bring a notebook. You'll have time to reflect and write when we're
there.

The students continue to prepare for their visit by learning more about the
Transcendentalism movement as well as the authors who were part of the
movement, and their works.

Writing About Literature

Later that semester, Ms. Wright returned to the issue of making comparisons within literary communities when she asked the students to do a 5- to 10-page research paper comparing two authors. She stressed many times that they were to write about things relevant to the authors' professional life and work, and to compare their styles.

This unit dovetailed with an essay Ms. Wright assigned calling upon Emerson's "Self-Reliance" and "Nature" and Thoreau's "Civil Disobedience" and segments from "Walden." Students used electronic and paper sources for information about Transcendentalism and looked for literary criticism related to poets/authors. For assistance in writing thesis statements, they referred to http://owl.english.purdue.edu/owl/resource/545/01/. For guidance in writing thesis statements, Ms. Wright suggested that they could turn a question into a provable statement and place it as the last sentence of the first paragraph. The students received a rubric to guide their planning and writing as well as to review the effectiveness of what they had written.

In this series of lessons, the students used both point-of-reference and horizons-of-possibilities orientations. When they read to get into and understand the poems or to gather ideas about the poems for reflection and writing at Walden Pond, their primary orientation involved exploring horizons of possibilities. However, when their primary focus during reading and discussion was on understanding Transcendentalism and when they compared writers, their orientations were primarily point of reference.

Ms. Wright also assigns compare-and-contrast essays to her 11th-graders. However, with them she offers more scaffolding that prepares them for their 12th-grade work. Her guide to completing compare-and-contrast research papers begins with a detailed explanation of the task:

> After conducting both book and electronic research, you will write a 5- to 10-page paper (excluding works cited page and title page) comparing/contrasting two literary figures you have chosen. You will examine their works, themes, styles, and awards. This paper will contain very little (if any) "life stuff." The reader doesn't care if the author had a dog named Fluffy when s/he was six. Your aim is to produce a comparison discussing the "literary lives" of your two authors, telling your reader what the authors' major works

are; what big themes they wrote about; what major influences they had; what major awards they won.

The guide goes on to explain that two sources are needed for each author, only one of which could be electronic, and to point them toward useful resources, both print and online. Finally, she provides a suggested outline for the paper, with seven sections that include attention to the writing style and major works of each author, similarities between their writing styles, differences between them, a recommendation on which author is "better" and why, and a conclusion about what has been learned. She also gives them an already completed paper with teacher comments to use as a model of what she expects.

Overall, you can see that in both 11th- and 12th-grade Honors English, Ms. Wright encourages her students to do a good deal of learning and thinking on their own, offering them scaffolding where she thinks they need it, often by suggesting websites or other means to locate the information they need and guidelines and models to follow. This, she feels, will prepare them for the independent work they will be expected to do when they attend college. However, she does offer them opportunities to work with one another in various kinds of collegial activities, minds-on and working together toward a common thoughtful goal. She also offers a good deal of in-class guidance and modeling to help students engage in literary discussion, including providing scaffolding for the content, language, and form that are appropriate.

Thus, Ms. Wright's class offers challenging material for students to read and opportunities to participate in an engaging oral discourse community, as well as to undertake challenging writing tasks appropriate to the discipline of literary study. Beyond providing activities that "up the ante" both conceptually and procedurally, she offers a range of scaffolds for students to use and nurtures their ability to reflect on, analyze, critique, and revise their own work.

ONLINE RESEARCH IN A SPECIAL EDUCATION CLASS

Laura Carroll, a special education teacher whose social studies lesson is described in Chapter 5, had her 8th-grade students read about elderly grandparents who are becoming more forgetful, using *Sachiko Means Happiness* by Kimiko Sakai (1990). First, they read and discuss the book, using the

"Idea Catcher" that Ms. Carroll developed. As described and illustrated in Chapter 5, the Idea Catcher is a sheet of paper folded origami-style into a "hat" that opens in four corners. Each open corner lists questions, based on the stances, for students to think about and discuss. Each student has his or her own Idea Catcher, and opens it to a section, reads the question, and tries to answer it before that same question is opened up for discussion.

Getting into the Text

Using the questions from the Idea Catcher, the students explore various aspects of their developing envisionment after reading. For example:

> *Question*: What is the turning point in the story? (Stance 2: Developing an Understanding of the Material)
> *Mark*: I just figured out the turning point. "I don't like the sunset." When my cat was dying with kidney failure, I gave her more company. . . .
> *Question*: How does this change the way you view the world? (Stance 3: Learning from the Material)
> *Jennifer*: Why they act that way. If someone acts that way you know they're old and sick. . . .

After a full discussion of the story, including taking perspectives from Sachiko and her grandmother's point of view, with Ms. Carroll guiding them, the students develop a concept map of the story.

Getting into the Topic

Following this, the students and Ms. Carroll begin to talk about Alzheimer's disease, a condition that the students had either heard about or had distant experience with. She then assigns them to do a web search for information about Alzheimer's. They take notes in their journals, writing down everything they think will help them understand the disease better. Then they meet to discuss what they learned, both individually and collectively. Through these various activities, the students are helped to broaden their envisionments of Alzheimer's, a central issue in the story.

Ms. Carroll then asks the students to return to *Sachiko Means Happiness* for evidence of noticeable characteristics of Alzheimer's that match with what the grandmother is saying or doing in the story. As the students match their new knowledge of Alzheimer's with what is said in the text, Ms. Carroll types their comments on the computer so they can see their comments on the overhead. Figure 8.1 shows the first page of what they produce.

And still they have not finished. Because they are quite engaged both in deepening their understanding of the story and learning about the disease, Ms. Carroll wants to help her students go even further and make more connections. Together, they turn the set of quotes and comments into a three-panel, fold-out brochure on the computer. After copies have been printed, they illustrate the story by hand. Then they practice enacting the story as a Reader's Theater, and write to the author about what they are doing. Meanwhile, Ms. Carroll contacts a local home for Alzheimer's patients and arranges for them all to visit. As a culminating activity, the students read to the patients, give them their brochures, and converse with them—as Sachiko had.

Figure 8.1. Students' Comments Relating Alzheimer's to the Story

Sachiko Young and Old: An Experience with Alzheimer's Disease

"I'm not Grandmother. I'm Sachiko 5 years old."

- Alzheimer's Disease affects a person's brain.

Sachiko was lost, frightened, scared, and along because she couldn't find her way home.

- People with Alzheimer's disease forget, have trouble speaking, sleeping, and taking care of themselves.

Sachiko was in tears because she was lost. "She turned to me. She was in tears." "I've never seen a grown-up cry."

- People with Alzheimer's disease get upset and frustrated easily.

"I looked into her eyes and tried to find the grandmother I once knew." "Slowly I began to understand. She is no longer Grandmother."

- As people get older their chances of getting Alzheimer's disease increases.

At the end of the story young Sachiko enjoyed the sunset because she understands the disease better and what her Grandmother is going through.

- You can't get Alzheimer's disease from another person like a cold or the flu. Just because someone has the disease it doesn't mean you will get it.

"Not Grandmother? Who is she then? Why does she say she is not Grandmother? Why does she say she should go home? Why does she make so much trouble for me?"

- Scientists don't know why people get Alzheimer's disease. There is no cure.

Young Sachiko takes her grandmother for a walk.

- People with Alzheimer's disease like to keep busy.

"I don't like sunsets, even if they are so beautiful. Trouble always comes in the evening. In the evening it always begins." Mother looked at me with relief. "Sachiko please talk with Grandmother for a while. I am busy preparing supper."

- Taking care of people with Alzheimer's disease is hard.

Young Sachiko shows she doesn't understand when she says, "Why should I take care of her?"

- People with Alzheimer's disease need to know you care. You may feel sad or angry about someone having the disease. It is important to remember that a person with Alzheimer's disease still loves you. Talk to people about the disease.

"Of course you can," I answered and grasped her hand tightly to reassure her, this little 5-year-old girl. Grandmother seemed uneasy. She patted her arm.

- When you hold their hand or give them a hug they will always feel your love.

Sachiko Means Happiness

Sachiko means happiness in Japanese. Both young and old Sachiko are happy because they can both enjoy the sunset together. Young Sachiko understands her Grandmother more. Old Sachiko is happier because she is loved and accepted as a friend, five years old.

During this activity, the students used both horizons-of-possibilities and point-of-reference orientations. When they read the story, they did so to better understand the characters, their relationships, the problem and the ways in which they dealt with it, why, and how they felt. These were developed primarily through a horizons-of-possibilities orientation. After reading and discussing this aspect of the story, they shifted to a point-of-reference orientation as they referred back to their research notes as well as the text to learn more about Alzheimer's, its symptoms and causes, and ways to interact with people who have the disease. Their learning went far beyond either understanding the story or gaining a deeper understanding of Alzheimer's disease. Their experiences with language and literacy (areas with which they have significant difficulty) enriched their repertoire of what was possible and gave them precedents for what they could do in the future, as well as practice in expressing themselves orally and in writing.

SUMMING UP

The three teachers described in this chapter engaged students in deepening their envisionments of literature as well as deepening their understanding of content related to the texts they read. The students also gained important language and literacy knowledge, in minds-on and cognitively interactive classrooms. Envisionment-building activities like these are appropriate for students at any ability level. The texts or content focus might be different, but the pedagogy would be the same. It is helpful for all students to be invited into an environment that is replete with thoughtful and engaging activities around challenging issues that are central to learning in English language arts. Class time is sufficiently interactive that although students begin by thinking about their own envisionments, they soon go beyond, learning from the range of material at their disposal as well as from the many thought-provoking activities. Although each of the teachers uses a wide range of approaches, including direct instruction and carefully selected scaffolding, the students bear responsibility for their own developing envisionments. They are guided in ways to become literate thinkers in English language arts, using language and form as well as content that are appropriate to the discipline.

Each of these classrooms is a cognitively active, personally exciting place where students, whatever their ability, are truly engaged with the ideas at hand and where they thoroughly enjoy their quest to know more. How do these teachers do it? They follow the four features of the envisioning-building classroom discussed in Chapter 4: build envisionments, forge curricular connections, orchestrate substantive and sustained discussion and writing, and offer enabling strategies.

Although everything I have discussed so far, in Chapters 1–8, can be undertaken by a teacher who is motivated to try the approach for their own professional growth, the biggest payoff to students in terms of knowledge growth, habits of mind, and test performance comes when there is a system-wide approach, where students have opportunities to engage in envisioning-building activities through their school day—day in and day out (Langer, 2004). How teachers interact with one another in ways that reinforce and advance student literacy through envisionment building is the focus of the next chapter.

CHAPTER 9

Envisionment Building Across Disciplines: Teachers Collaborating in a Professional Community

In previous chapters we met two envisionment-building teachers—Monica Judd, a science teacher, and Randall Roeser, a teacher of mathematics who taught in the same school. Now we will look at the professional community that they and their colleagues developed to enable them to grow professionally and to help their students grow academically. They wanted to emphasize literate thinking, envisionment building, and minds-on instruction as a way to infuse critical thinking into their students' daily classroom experiences. "Team 82" is made up of four grade 8 core subject teachers, one in each of the subjects, who together are responsible for a designated cohort of students. Organizationally, the team is not unlike many middle school teams in the United States, except that this group's members formed themselves into an unusually active and ongoing collaborative professional community. In addition to Judd and Roeser, the group also included Laurie Farina, an English language arts teacher, and David Ackley, a social studies teacher (he moved to this team at the beginning of its second year, when another social studies teacher retired).

Soon after they began their collaborative work, they tried to set out their goals. After some discussion, Ms. Farina, the English teacher, sent this email to the others:

> Hey guys,
>   I've typed up the goals for your perusal. Also, for the next meeting we were going to come with ideas for a survey to administer to students to find out what they know at the beginning of the year, keeping in mind our goal of having measurable goals!

Also, read part three of Eija's book [Adler & Rougle, 2005] and all of the other one [Langer, 1995] especially with a thought to making some essential questions at the meeting too.
Whew!
Laurie

These are the goals she sent them:

Learning Goals

Students will:

- Create a community of learners by collaborating with one another and engaging others in dialogue as well as allowing new ideas to develop their own thinking.
- Make content connections, while reading and discussing, with prior knowledge course content, personal experiences, current events, etc. . . .
- Use evidence and examples to support claims or arguments.
- Use many strategies to learn, such as discussion, writing, construction, experimentation, and communication.
- Form thinking habits that question ideas and information so that students may understand more deeply.

Instructional Goals (Rough)

- Team-wide consistency, use of common academic vocabulary [as well as use of particular disciplinary vocabulary], consistent high expectations for critical thinking
- Enthusiasm for subject
- Overtly model critical thinking [in our subject areas] for students
- Promote good dialogic conversation by providing valuable opportunities
- Scaffold student learning to allow the gradual release of responsibility for students to use the knowledge on their own, while we help with new and more difficult concepts and strategies

These goals were not Ms. Farina's alone. They represented what the team had been discussing during team meetings as well as a 2-day summer retreat.

Before Team 82 began their collaborative project, a number of ELA teachers in their school and district had been part of the Partnership for Literacy (P4L), a 2-year research project funded by the Institute of Education Sciences and directed by Arthur Applebee, Martin Nystrand, and myself. The study was designed to help teachers focus on the concepts about learning and teaching discussed in Chapters 2–4, within an interacting professional network. The emphasis was on ways to develop students' literate minds and critical-thinking abilities associated with learning and achievement and to track teacher and student change across 2 years.

Project activities zeroed in on the participating teachers' professional knowledge, as well as their understandings of what their students knew, giving them agency to do their work, while offering them a pedagogical framework and guidance to continue their own professional growth (Langer, Applebee, & Nystrand, 2005). By the end of 2 years, the P4L students had been so successful that when the students moved on to other teachers, the effects of the project seemed obvious. As one teacher put it, "I can tell a Partnership student right away. They dig beneath the surface and try to come up with more sophisticated understandings." As a result, both administrators and teachers of other subjects wanted to become part of the Partnership, even after the original research project had come to a close. Thus, they became members of the Partnership for Literacy professional development program that followed.

The district's assistant superintendent for instruction, who had a participatory management style and took a "bubble-up" approach to instructional change, supported those teachers who wished to opt in to envisionment building rather than mandating this approach across the board.

Before Team 82 began collaborating, Ms. Farina was one of the English teachers who had already joined the Partnership for Literacy, and she had shared her enthusiasm for its approaches with her colleagues. It was in this way, as result of their own professionalism and desire to improve their students' achievement, that Team 82, a group of four middle school teachers who had no history of instructional collaboration, became involved— hook, line, and sinker. Their goal was to do interdisciplinary planning (not interdisciplinary teaching), so that their 8th-grade students would experience common goals and approaches as they moved from class to class across the school day. They wanted all their classes to embrace the features of the envisionment-building classroom, while fine-tuning it to the different content, concepts, language, and ways of thinking that were central to each of their disciplines. They wanted to connect their different courses with a unified and overarching pedagogy and approach to teaching.

To do this, they worked together with Eija Rougle, a Partnership instructional facilitator, who continued to work in their district with the "bubble-up" teachers. Dr. Rougle had worked for many years in the research projects that led up to the Partnership, and continues, along with a growing team of instructional facilitators, to help make the ideas described in these chapters a reality. While she helped Team 82 faculty refine their understandings of the pedagogy and teaching approaches that are central to envisionment-building classrooms, they brought the disciplinary knowledge and knowledge of their students to make it work. It was the teamwork, collegial professional growth, and commitment that made them so effective. In fact, when the Team 82 social studies position became available, Mr. Ackley requested a transfer from another team in the same school in order to become part of the group's work. Let's look at some of the things they did.

COMING TOGETHER

All teachers in the school knew about the successes of the Partnership for Literacy teachers and students. Well before they formed their own professional community, Team 82 teachers had seen and spoken about the positive effects on the successive groups of students they had seen moving from grade 7 Partnership classes to grade 8. "In fact," Mr. Roeser said, "by the time we began our collaboration, only two [of our] students were not Partnership alums before starting." Team 82 wanted to build on the kinds of critical thinking the students had already learned to do, and to implement the activities on a systematic basis across all subjects.

In addition to team meetings in the spring semester, they requested and were granted a paid planning retreat to take place the second week in August. This was to be repeated as part of a larger summer Partnership institute in each of the following 3 years, if not beyond. (This book is being written at the end of Year 3.)

Summer Retreat

The first full-length planning retreat was particularly successful; it was here that the team members set the ground rules, goals, and procedures they would follow for the next 3, now going on 4, years. The main purpose of the two summer planning days was to develop a mission and vision for themselves. Although it was to be relevant to the district mission, the specific task they set themselves was to develop Team 82 Learning Goals that would enhance their teaching of literate and critical thinking in their classrooms and also to develop collegial discourse among themselves. They wanted to increase their own capacities in teaching literate thinking in their subjects. Together, they agreed to develop pedagogical tools (concepts, activities, and strategies for teaching them), share what they had done, and engage in ongoing personal and collaborative reflective practice. Further, because they wanted to be confident that their work was having a positive effect on student learning, they planned to develop measurable goals, as well as have ongoing collaborative renegotiation of how to best reach those goals. Thus, from the beginning, the teachers reflected on and discussed their own experiences and looked to professional literature for ideas to move them ahead on their goals. Their focus was always on how to translate the ideas into helping their students gain greater control of their own thinking and improve their subject-area learning.

Certain procedures were set up for that first year. They decided to meet regularly to discuss their own teaching and reflect on what they were doing. They also asked Dr. Rougle to bring articles and engage them in activities that would move ahead their own thinking about minds-on classrooms and students' critical thinking. The first year was devoted primarily to developing a common understanding of effective envisionment-building classrooms across disciplines, through study, discussion, and reflection.

YEAR 1: DEVELOPING PROBLEM-BASED, MINDS-ON ACTIVITIES

Throughout the first year, Team 82 continued to meet regularly, for 40 minutes, during their team time. At their early meetings, they talked about the Partnership for Literacy framework and strategies for learning through envisionment building—what it means and how to create it in their subjects. This included developing problem-based and other minds-on activities where students need to do research or experiments using discipline-specific approaches, language, and ways of thinking. They also developed ways to help the students reflect on processes and products, and explored the roles discussion, writing, and technology could play in thinking about and learning the content.

Introducing Guidelines for Discussion

One of their early products was a list of guidelines for how to have a thought-provoking and substantive discussion about course content, within the boundaries of each discipline. They discussed the list with their students, then posted it in a noticeable place in each room, to be referred to during discussion time. It said:

- Be respectful of others' opinions, but maintain your own if it holds up.
- Pay attention: Face everyone, make eye contact, listen to what others have to say, have positive body language (nodding your head, posture, don't fidget).
- No sidebars.
- Be prepared to have something to say.
- Stay within the boundaries of the topic of discussion, build on others' ideas, make connections, ask questions, offer different viewpoints, or tell why you agree.
- Speak loudly and clearly and minimize "like" and "um."
- Don't be afraid to speak your mind, but don't hog the discussion.
- Explain and defend your point of view. Give examples and comparisons.
- Take turns politely. Don't raise your hand.
- Take notes to save your ideas until you have a turn.

Because the students already had been acculturated into thoughtful discourse communities, the list ended up being a more important activity for the teachers than for the students. It helped them think through what to expect, look for, and encourage. Before long, discussions in all four classes were more participatory than in previous classes, with true back-and-forth conversations among classmates who questioned initial statements, defended interpretations, and added new ideas. Conversations became discipline-appropriate learning events, like those presented in Chapters 5–8. Delighted with the students' level of thought and understanding, the teachers worked harder to analyze their own lessons and gain the comfort to have minds-on classes every day, as a matter of course.

Team meetings were also a time when Dr. Rougle or one of the four teachers would bring in an article for all to read or hear about—one related to instructional issues with which they were grappling, meaty enough to engage them in substantive professional discussion and reflection, and thought-provoking enough to help further their own professional development.

Incorporating Technology

Although the first year was primarily a time for study, reflection, discussion, and planning, Ms. Farina, who already had incorporated some of the envisionment-building strategies into her classes, wanted to begin to incorporate computers into the content-based, minds-on activities in her classroom. The school had several full-class sets of computers that were on carts that could be rolled into particular classrooms at particular times. (The school has wireless Internet and intranet access.) She arranged to have the cart available for all her 8th-grade English classes, and the students used them for their journals, drafting, composing, peer editing, and revision. Students worked in groups of four or five to do peer editing of one another's works, using the "commenting" and "track changes" tools in Microsoft Word to facilitate the revision of shared documents.

The entire class also used the discussion area in Blackboard to interact about what they were studying, including discussions of content, form, and style. Ms. Farina checked on the discussions and used the technology to communicate with individual students, entire groups, or at times the entire class—offering suggestions, models, or references that would help them focus more, go deeper, make connections, or go beyond. In these ways, she used the computer as a tool to stimulate students' manipulation of content appropriate to the study of language and literature, extending their envisionments and enriching their knowledge.

During spring of this first year, and in both fall and spring of the successive years, Team 82 attended a district-wide Partnership for Literacy professional development conference, to which each teacher brought evidence of his or her most successful disciplinary lesson(s) for teachers across the subjects to discuss and learn from.

YEAR 2: ENHANCING CRITICAL THINKING THROUGH WRITING

Reflecting

Toward the end of their first year, Team 82 reflected on the year and planned for the next. Overall, they were pleased that they were well under way to developing a common view of behaviors and strategies demonstrated by good students, including ways in which to more systematically engage them in higher-order thinking as they moved from class to class across the school day. This included a common vocabulary for minds-on reading, writing, and discussion strategies that cut across the subjects and could be used in class to offer a coherent message to students. Aware that they needed more time to meet and plan, the team asked their principal to let them combine their team time and planning periods to allow them to meet for 80 minutes at a time. Pleased with student and teacher progress, the principal consented.

Planning

After school had closed, the team members emailed one another about planning for next year's instruction and their own professional needs. In July, after Mr. Roeser had reflected on the last few meetings they had had before the school year ended, he wrote this to the team:

> Hi,
>
>   I hope everyone is enjoying the summer.
>
>   You may have seen the attached article on critical thinking in the most recent *American Educator* [Willingham, 2007]. Timely, I thought, with respect to our conversations on June 25. I found this article sobering, but helpful. The main points I took away are:
>
> a.   We need to tie critical thinking closely to the content of our curricula. In other words, we need to be giving students opportunities to talk and write critically about the subject matter they are learning right then and there.
> b.   We need to do a lot of modeling of critical thinking in our disciplines.
> c.   We need to give students lots of practice, not only with using critical thinking but, metacognitively, making decisions about when to employ critical thinking.

Although from the beginning the teachers had focused on developing critical thinking in their students, they responded to this email and article by deciding to take a closer look and ask themselves, "What do I mean by critical thinking in my discipline?"

They jotted their responses and then had a discussion about the differences and overlaps. Overall, their notions of critical thinking included cognitive moves such as comparing, analyzing, synthesizing, explaining, justifying, and evaluating. They knew this would be an ongoing task for them, but they also decided that it would be important for their students to do the same exercise—at the beginning and end of the year. That way, as a team, they could reflect on the kinds of thinking they were assigning and the students were doing.

Surveying Students on Critical Thinking. With a renewed focus on critical thinking, the teachers told their students about their joint focus on critical thinking and developed tasks from each of the four disciplines that invited students to engage in it. Thus, from the beginning, the students were aware of the focus on critical thinking and were also treated as important partners who provided feedback that would be useful in the teachers' planning. In October, the team administered a critical-thinking survey to every student in their classes. One class period was used. Examples of student responses are listed below each question (see bullets).

Critical-Thinking Survey

As you may remember from the beginning of the year, Team 82 teachers are working on some research to improve our teaching. We would like your help. Please give us your best thoughts on the following questions.

Examples of written comments follow:

What does a critical thinker in a social studies class do?

- Not just learn information, but think how history has affected or relates to today
- Compares the situation to other times and the present day? What else could have been done? Also always asking "so what?"
- In social studies you always need to go beyond knowledge, you need to compare/contrast, change, what could be different, better, who, what when, where, why, how.
- In social studies a critical thinker looks at different view points and also at the way the times and culture affected what happened.

What does a critical thinker in a science class do?

- Find out how or why something works. Develop a way to test different parts to learn how they affect what you're looking at.

- You need to analyze why everything happens, what would happen if you changed something, added or took away a verible (sic).
- Ask themselves: How are experiments related? Why do things outside of science happen?
- Thinks about how this is used in actual life.

What does a critical thinker in a math class do?

- Not only doing the problem, understanding why you do it that way.
- Connect one method of solving to another to find new ways to solve/evaluate it.
- Thinks about how to make a problem simpler and different ways to answer it.
- Wonder what if, try new ways, discover new methods, challenge old theories, try many techniques from different angles.

What does a critical thinker in an English class do?

- They go beyond the words on the paper and analyze what they have thought. Look at other points of view.
- Try and get a deeper meaning of something they're reading. Also they try to think about things they read and write in a more creative/expressive way.
- They look behind the words of something. They don't take things literally. They are thinking about connections, questions, and predictions.
- Reads and thinks. Think of what you read. What would be different in real life? What else could have happened? Look up important information in class and compare it to the book. Tries to put themselves in the idea or a book. Goes deeper to learn more.

Thinking about your past experience, in what way does class discussion help you to learn more or to understand more?

- It gets you to think about ideas in a different way. Class discussion also lets you hear what other people think and helps you develop ideas more.
- If you don't understand something, you may understand it after discussion. You can change your ideas for the better, too.

- In class discussions a lot of different people talk, so you can learn more about how you can look at something in a different way, and you might learn something you didn't catch before.
- It helps me organize the info in my head better.

Describe one writing experience (not necessarily this year) when you felt you were a really good critical thinker.

- We did an essay in Ms. XX's class about Native Americans. I think a way I was a critical thinker is because of her way of us going about it with Think Charts. I did really well because I got all the details to support what I thought and to make comparisons and what I thought was really critical.
- The soda can reflection—looked in depth at what was happening—used evidence, made inferences, came to a conclusion, and then had to explain why. She didn't tell us how it happened or why; we had to think critically.
- I felt like a critical thinker in my "Waterfall" entry. I went deeper (literally!) and described my five senses. I described what I felt like, etc. [had to find the right language].
- Once we wrote a reflection on a pendulum in math. In that I really analyzed what happened.

Student responses helped the teachers become aware that they would need to become even more explicit about helping students gain awareness of discipline-appropriate critical thinking and speaking.

The team also began to focus on the relative cognitive demands of the various tasks, trying to identify those that demanded more higher-level thinking, aware that it can be and should be part and parcel of their concern for critical thinking. They wanted to be certain that the course activities, assignments, and discussions were sufficiently cognitively challenging and that the students could recognize and learn to control their level of thinking as they read, wrote, and spoke about the content, as appropriate for the task. For example, they wanted their students to be able to write rubrics identifying the characteristics of a well-organized analysis, a well-defended argument, a well-connected construct, or a well-justified evaluation and to apply them to their own coursework.

The team also decided to share videos of their lessons and copies of student work, this time with a major focus on critical thinking. Unlike most professional development programs, they were very much orchestrating their own learning and developing their own plans, using Dr. Rougle as a professional resource.

The team decided to focus on discussion as a way to make students' thinking visible to the students as well as the teachers. The teachers focused their own learning on how to ask thought-provoking questions and how to offer appropriate scaffolding and direct instruction at points of need as a way to help their students learn to engage in substantive and conceptually interactive discussions. They created a chart that identified three levels of critical thinking:

1. Statements of facts and descriptions
2. Connections, comparisons and contrasts, analyses, explanations, justifications, classifications
3. Generalizations, evaluations, and more fully developed and defended critiques

Team 82 agreed that at each meeting they would take turns presenting a lesson that they had given that involved substantive discussion, one that had pleased them or one that they had questions about. In each case, they would expect and welcome discussion and feedback.

Enacting

As this second year began, the team had a core of common goals, approaches, activities, and ways of interacting with their students in place, as well as a bank of material to use. For their meetings, each teacher generally videotaped the lesson they wanted to discuss, and also brought in related student work for their colleagues to discuss. Following procedures that had been developed in the Partnership (Rodgers, 2002), the teacher whose lesson was being studied would give a brief introduction, and then the team would watch a selected segment, first focusing on the teacher—what the teacher was doing, asking, assigning, and what the content focus was. (This technique was introduced to them by Dr. Rougle, and soon came to be used regularly.) During a second viewing, they would focus on the students—what they were doing and asking, the content the students were thinking about, and the ways in which they were thinking about it. During a third viewing, they would look at the materials, activities, and tools being used. Last, they would look at the entire video to see how these human and material dimensions interacted to create a thought-provoking disciplinary environment for the students. For example, how engaged were students in thinking through disciplinary concepts with discipline-appropriate language? To what end were they using critical-thinking strategies?

This in-depth look at the lesson as an interactive learning environment helped them see relationships between their own activities, actions, questions, interactions, scaffolding, and expectations and their students' opportunities to become engaged with the concepts and language of the course. They also sometimes discussed whole lessons with these perspectives in mind. Thus, each team meeting became a time for growth, for each of the four teachers, no matter whose lesson they were discussing.

At the beginning of this second year, Mr. Ackley joined the team. In response to now working with students who had been in Ms. Polsinelli's class the year before (see Chapter 5), he said, "They came with life grids and were trained as historians." He was highly motivated to catch up with his colleagues; at the same time, his presence offered the rest of the team a time to reflect on their own assumptions, behaviors, and expectations.

Thinking and Writing as Historians. Mr. Ackley's class, for example, did a unit on the Reconstruction period in American history. In this class, we can see how the team's interest in discussion worked together with their interest in critical thinking to deepen students' explorations of new concepts within each subject. Working toward an end-of-unit essay on "How Radical Was the Reconstruction?," he had his students read several articles written from various viewpoints, as well as the relevant sections of their textbook. Here is a brief part of an early discussion, to provide a sense of the way his questions model issues that students, thinking as historians, need to consider.

> *Meg*: It was a white Southerner who wrote this. . . .
> *Mr. Ackley*: What red flags are there that concern you?
> *Louis*: Here it puts Johnson in a good light, but not in the textbooks. . . .
> *Mr. Ackley*: Why did the Northerners have to get involved?
> *Students*: Loopholes in the Constitution, couldn't vote, poll tax, literacy test. . . .
> *Mr. Ackley*: Why would it make a difference when it was written?
> *Robert*: Historians look back at history, and they sometimes change their views.

During their reading of the multiple texts, Mr. Ackley asked the students to use a variety of readers' marks (annotations in the margins of the text) to highlight their developing understanding, such as:

- Underlining what they thought was important or unexpected
- Putting a question mark next to something they didn't understand
- Putting a *C* next to something to which they made a connection
- Putting an *I* next to an inference they were making that was not said directly
- Putting a star next to something they'd like to come back to as an interesting quote or piece of information

They also did a "stand and deliver" activity, where they had to take different sides and put forth a convincing oral argument for the side they chose. Then, in preparation for writing the essay, they responded in writing to the following:

1. What have you learned from the readings (new information, questions, connections)?
2. Looking at the events, issues, and people from the perspective of the time in which they occurred, what new insights/old insights and connections do you have about the Reconstruction effort?

Through discussion, students clustered their various responses to the above questions, prioritized them based on their perceived importance, and interrelated them in ways that showed hierarchical connections. This provided them with an opportunity not only to make judgments about the salience of various data and ideas they had read in terms of Reconstruction, but also to make connections between and among ideas and build a fuller construct. The activities Mr. Ackley chose were motivated by his desire to help his students think like historians, including taking into account issues of historical time and differing points of view. He felt this, and other thought-provoking lessons like it throughout the year, would help his students do better on their state exam as well as in class. Students said Mr. Ackely's activities helped them add depth to their essays and also improved their exam writing.

Team 82 also extended their focus on critical thinking to writing as well as discussion. For example, each teacher prepared a statement called

"Why Write in (Math, Social Studies, Science, English)." This was used to stimulate discussion about writing in each of the subject classes. Mr. Roeser's version is displayed in Figure 9.1.

Figure 9.1. Why Write in Math?

ARE YOU LOOKING TO START AN ARGUMENT? GOOD!

Why write in math?

You will be asked to write often in math class this year. When I say "writing," I mean sentences and paragraphs that express your thoughts and ideas about the mathematics that you are learning. You will write in different places: in your class notes, on quizzes and tests, and in this Math Journal. Writing in math benefits you in several ways:

- Writing about math helps you organize and clarify your thinking. In other words, having put your ideas in writing actually helps you learn.
- Writing gives you and opportunity to use specific math vocabulary.
- Writing—and especially the kind of writing you will do in this Math Journal—will give you practice crafting *mathematical arguments*. In a mathematical argument, you state a conclusion, prediction, or conjecture and then support your position using mathematical facts and principles. Over the course of the year, I expect you to become increasingly proficient at writing mathematical arguments. This Math Journal will help you and your readers track your progress.

How will your writing be evaluated?

Your writing in this Math Journal will be evaluated like your writing in other team subjects. The reader will be looking to see how well you do the following:

- Clearly state a position (a conclusion, prediction, or conjecture).
- Justify (support) your position by providing solid reasoning based on mathematical facts and principles.
- Use specific math vocabulary.

In addition to the three criteria above, you can enhance your mathematical arguments by doing the following:

- Make connections—to other mathematics that you have learned, to other subjects, or to topics outside of school.
- Reflect on your writing: Ask "wonder" questions, tell about things that still puzzle you, discuss an implication of what you have written.

Discussing and Writing in Math. Immediately after discussing "Why Write in Math" with his students, Mr. Roeser gave them the following writing prompt to respond to: "*A student wrote $2^3 = 6$ on his homework. Convince the student that he is wrong.*" It stimulated good explanatory thinking and writing about multiplication, powers, and exponents.

Early in the school year, Mr. Roeser posed the Border Problem for the students to do as part of their work to understand variable expressions and to begin to develop their algebraic thinking skills. As did other members of the team, he wove discussion and writing together around a cognitively challenging task. Mr. Roeser began by showing his students a 10x10 grid, with the following assignment: "Without counting one-by-one, figure out how many unit squares are in the border of a 10x10 grid. Find at least one way to represent your method arithmetically." There was a good deal of discussion as students suggested different ways to calculate the number of unit squares in the border, defended their solutions, and questioned one another. (For one discussion of the Border Problem, see www.doe.mass.edu/Sumit/StrengtheningMath.pdf.) Throughout, Mr. Roeser provided feedback and scaffolding to keep the discussion going, such as "Defend yourself," or "I see a direction that is profitable [keep with it]," or "What's your computation now?"

The students generated a total of six valid methods for computing the border. Each method was described using a numerical expression that worked for the 10x10 grid. Mr. Roeser chose one student's method and led the class through a process of generalization, beginning with a geometric or visual representation of the method, leading to a verbal representation, and finally an algebraic representation in the form of a variable expression. Students were then challenged to use that method to compute (more quickly and easily) the border of a different-size grid, thus demonstrating the power of algebraic thinking. For homework, Mr. Roeser asked the students to come up with geometric, verbal, and algebraic representations for the remaining five methods. The following day, the students compared their representations in small groups and could revise what they had done.

To complete their work for the Border Problem, students were asked to reflect on their work using the following prompt:

As the final item in your portfolio, please answer the questions below that will help you summarize what you have learned from the Border Problem.

1. List the variable expressions that you wrote for the six different methods.

    a. How are the variable expressions all alike?
    b. Write your own definition of "variable expression."
    c. Which one of the variable expressions do you think is the most "simplified?" Why?

2. An important goal of the Border Problem was to show you how variable expressions can be used to describe a pattern. Which of the other three representations, numerical expressions, geometric drawing or verbal, was most helpful to you in coming up with the variable expression for each student's method. Why?

At the outset of the investigation, Mr. Roeser had given the students a rubric for scoring the Border Problem. The first parts of the rubric gave specific points for each of the solutions for correct numerical expressions, accurate geometric drawings, complete and correct verbal description, and a correct variable expression. The final section of the rubric concerned the two questions in the reflection above:

Writing Guidelines

*   You may write your reflection by hand (legibly) or use a word processor.
*   Proofread your writing.
*   Your writing will be scored on the following four elements:
    Completeness (3 points): Did you answer both questions completely, including the "why" questions?
    Understanding (3 points): Does your writing show a good understanding of the mathematics in the Border Problem?
    Vocabulary (3 points): Did you use specific and accurate mathematical vocabulary and avoid vague terms like "it"?
    Mechanics (3 points): Did you write complete sentences and use capitalization and end-of-sentence punctuation?

In the Border Problem reflection task and its accompanying rubric, we see how thoroughly Mr. Roeser is engaging his students in using multiple representations of their evolving mathematical knowledge to add depth and sophistication to their envisionments of disciplinary concepts.

Throughout the year, discussion was used in each of the classes as a way to help students think about and learn the course content. While critical thinking was a goal, small- and large-group discussion, as well as writing, were used to add depth to the knowledge the students were developing. Overall, each of the teachers' approaches changed dramatically over the first 2 years, with an increased focus on their students' growing ability to think flexibly as well as deeply as they built understandings of subject-area knowledge and its connections to the larger world. Beyond that, the teachers were becoming adept at planning activities and supporting discussions that moved their students to communicate in increasingly more discipline-appropriate ways.

YEAR 3: LEARNING AND THINKING MORE DEEPLY IN THE DISCIPLINES

Planning

As the school year came to a close, Mr. Roeser wrote a note to the district administrator who was overseeing the continuing Partnership for Literacy involvement, and to Dr. Rougle. You will see that his concern, like theirs, continues to be on using the envisionment-building pedagogy to help students learn and think more deeply about their course content. Clearly, he intended his email to be a discussion starter.

> Dear Eija and Gail,
>
>   I took time today to compose some ideas for what our team's literacy initiatives might look like next year. I did this primarily to help sort out my own thinking, but thought I might share them with you ahead of time.
>
>   I haven't shared them with my colleagues. I am all too well aware of the power of the written word. I'm afraid if I presented this document as a draft proposal, it could limit our thinking and perhaps lead us in a direction the others might not agree with. But if you think it appropriate to present it at our meeting, that's fine.
>
>   See you Monday at 9:00.

Literacy Goals for Team 82

Student Outcomes

Over the course of the year, students will demonstrate increasing proficiency at:

1. Presenting oral and written arguments for scrutiny by others that are supported by evidence and sound reasoning (e.g., justification, inductive reasoning, proof).
2. Using the formal vocabulary of the discipline in speaking and writing.
3. Contributing to class discussions that deepen and enrich the discussion and their understanding of the content.
4. Reflecting on their learning.

Instructional Strategies

To support achievement of the student outcomes, the team teachers will:

1. Use common ground rules and phrases for class discussions.
2. Share a set of core strategies for initiating and extending class discussions and students thinking.
3. Use a common set of text marks and a common rubric for assessing student writing.
4. Explicitly model the vocabulary and thinking habits of our respective disciplines.
5. Have students write on extended prompts at least ____ times per week.
6. Assess the writing of students in the core subjects other than our own and invite outsiders to assess their writing.
7. Observe each others' classes and the classes of other teachers using [Partnership] strategies.

Things to Ponder

1. Does it make sense to have students use a common journal or compile a team-wide portfolio of writing?
2. How can Blackboard be used by all teachers to support our literacy goals?
3. Will we have to cut back on content in order to give adequate attention to our literacy goals?

4. Can we use Flex as a more direct extension of our classes to make more time for literacy?

Because the team wanted to engage the students in thoughtful and discipline-appropriate writing as well as discussion that would support critical thinking, they decided to ask students to do a wide variety of writing, from journal jots and note-taking through explanations of thoughts, processes, and understandings, as well as reflections on what they had done.

The team also decided to have students keep portfolios of their writing in order to track growth in their thinking and understanding of subject-area content knowledge across the year. Thus, early in the year, the team developed a rubric to be used by the students as well as themselves (see Chapter 7, Figure 7.4). Although they developed a generic rubric that applied across disciplines, the teachers often personalized it to the particular course content.

To continue and enhance their own professional development, the team also committed to weekly meetings, instead of the biweekly sessions that had been more typical in the first 2 years.

Engaging in an Extended I-Search Activity

During Year 3, Ms. Farina involved her students in an extended I-Search activity (Macrorie, 1988). She wanted it to be on a topic about which the students themselves were curious. After identifying a topic and getting Ms. Farina's approval, students used information gleaned from primary as well as secondary sources, including interviews, the Internet, print, and other material. They then wrote about what they had found as well as about their I-Search experience. The four-phase body of work took 10 weeks to complete. Phase One involved the students in identifying the topic and posing the question. During this phase, Ms. Farina gave a number of mini-lessons on writing business letters and email inquiries in search of information. Phase Two involved planning the search. This was the time when students identified possible contacts, developed an I-Search plan, submitted rough drafts of letters and emails, and developed a list of interview questions. During this second phase, Ms. Farina gave several mini-lessons on evaluating web sources (e.g., she used "The Good, the Bad, and the Ugly," from the New Mexico State University Library website, http://lib.nmsu.edu/).

Phase Three involved the actual searching. In addition to taking careful notes and citing sources, students were expected to evaluate their sources, conduct interviews, and do a post-interview reflection for each. Due dates were established for rough drafts of sections discussing their topic, their plan, and their search. Phase Four involved completion of the paper (on both what they had learned about the topic and what they had learned about doing research), including peer-group editing, followed by presentations.

Throughout the 10 weeks, Ms. Farina helped the students focus on higher-level questions, to think about what they found in more interesting ways, and to write about their topic in depth. The nature of the task allowed her to work with each of the students, whatever their previous experience and comfort with the task. She helped them to research a topic they cared about, to get cognitively involved in the search, to approach each set of tasks with greater depth of thought, and to report what they had learned in a more highly literate and more thoughtfully written presentation.

CONTINUING SELF-STUDY

To assist in their own professional growth, each teacher made a videotape of at least one extended discussion, and the team developed a rubric for evaluating the level of thinking students exhibited during the discussion, and discussed how to "up the ante" to encourage more higher-order thinking.

During other team meetings, they focused on how such thinking was reflected in students' writing. One teacher would explain a lesson and distribute the substantive student writing associated with that body of work (brief activities such as journal jots or notes were not reviewed). Then all teachers jointly read and evaluated the writing using the team rubric. The focus on critical thinking from an envisionment-building perspective continued throughout the year.

To aid in their own self-study, toward the end of the year, Team 82 asked their students to compile a "Cumulative Portfolio on Critical Thinking" across the four core subjects. In addition to including work from the entire year, students were asked to write a reflection on the critical thinking they had done across the year in each subject, and to revise one previously written piece, with attention to higher-level thought given to the topic. Thus, students were expected to engage in metacognitive reflection, and use it to revise or rethink their earlier work, having "upped the ante" of their own critical thought. The team used the students' comments to help them refine their own teaching. For example, the team concluded that "We also needed to be more intentional about illuminating for our students the similarities in thinking across the disciplines." (See the wiki that Team 82 developed about this project at http://criticalthinking8thgrade.wikispaces.com.)

They also became aware of the need for a greater focus on writing as a "medium for getting at the development of students' thinking." (See their wiki section titled "Action Research.")

As part of their own self-study, the teachers selected 12 students, with an equal mix of high, average, and low performers as well as girls and boys. These students' written work was examined and evaluated at the team meetings. In addition, at the end of the year, each student was interviewed and videotaped while reflecting on his or her own critical-thinking experiences. The meetings were informal and interactive, which allowed the teachers to probe the students' responses and for the students to speak conversationally. The teachers analyzed the comments and used them as another way to reflect on their own teaching and to stimulate their joint planning for the next year. Here is an example of a self-evaluation that Ms. Farina wrote:

> The use of the rubric + other accompanying marks [e.g., reader's marks] by teachers, have greatly improved students' critical thinking and, more importantly, awareness of their own critical thinking.
>
> Next year I can do a better job of using model papers and examples of critical thinking for students to see and internalize. Also, in speaking with students in the portfolio process, I need to give students a clear definition of what critical thinking is in English, as well as examples from their own papers.
>
> Try to create a better community of learners where the topic of discussion is also "Is this critical thinking?"

As you can see, by the end of the third year, Team 82 had a cycle of continual reflection and self-improvement firmly in place. Time and again, they focused on their own teaching, on their students' performance, and on the ways these interact to enhance students' conceptual understanding of the material. This kind of professional and instructional improvement cycle is a mark of more effective programs (Langer, 2001). Team 82 has more work to do, and they have already begun to plan next year's work. Wider use of technology to stimulate critical thinking within their disciplinary contexts is one of their goals.

SUMMING UP

Team 82 is a very rare example of how well teachers across disciplines can work collaboratively as a professional community to enhance teaching and learning for all students. They know that learning, for teachers and for students, never stops; it is an ongoing process. When the team began, they were quite aware that there are disciplinary differences in ways to solve problems, present evidence, discuss, write, and otherwise develop knowledge. They were also aware that there is an overlap, an academic language and approaches to teaching and learning that cut across the disciplines that could "provide our students with a powerful and coherent literacy experience." (See the wiki sections titled "Action Research Plan" and "History of Our Action Research.") They took on this task with full awareness that their classes are mainstreamed classes with students representing a wide range of abilities and needs. The goal was to help all students learn to think more critically and productively as they gain knowledge and literacy in their disciplines. Across the 3 years, the students did, in fact, become more active thinkers whose envisionments of subject-area concepts grew wider and deeper.

Clearly, Team 82 sees itself as having begun an ongoing quest toward professional growth and improvement in student achievement. This model of team effort is especially strong because it establishes a common pedagogical framework, yet fine-tunes it to the needs of their particular classes, their school and district priorities, and their own negotiated goals. With this as a starting place, instructional goals and activities are closely attuned to student needs. As a matter of course, the teachers keep up with related professional literature, discussing and critiquing it from their own envisionment-building perspective.

Because they are a professional team that shares the same students, this collaboration is especially effective; it ensures that each of their students will experience a consistently supportive envisionment-building environment as she or he moves from class to class across the school day, throughout the year. During each year that Team 82 has worked together, more and more teachers in the school have asked to engage in Partnership activities. Some work within their own teams and some work in content-area clusters. Thus, although no other teachers can join Team 82, Dr. Rougle helps these other teachers form their own professional groups. They are eager to do this, they say, because the students are more enthusiastic about their learning, think more deeply, and learn more extensively. After several years, as more and more teachers participated in this larger Partnership for Literacy effort, they were not at all surprised to see that in addition to students' increasing engagement in their coursework, the school scores on high-stakes tests also improved.

Could the instructional program have changed faster and could the students have made academic gains more rapidly with a more typical top-down mandated approach to professional development? Would it have been as successful in professionalizing the teachers or improving the knowledge and literacy of the students involved? As a reader who has reached the end of Chapter 9, you know my envisionment-building and minds-on perspective. It holds for people of all ages. As I discuss in my book *Getting to Excellent* (Langer, 2004), my studies show that schools that are most successful over the long run are those with professional communities such as Team 82. Such communities grow from teachers' thirst for more professional knowledge as they address the problems they and their students are facing. This puts them in the position of being professional knowledge builders—professionals who identify their own problems, keep in touch with current research in their fields, and use what they learn to fine-tune their own teaching in ways that meet their own local needs— those of their school, district, community, and students.

CHAPTER 10

Closing the Circle:
The Role of Literacy in
Disciplinary Knowledge

I cannot end this book without a return to the central questions I raised as I began Chapter 1: What is knowledge? How do we gain it? How do we teach it? The answers are extremely important. Not only do students' schoolwork and test performance depend on them, but so does the future shape of our world. What we consider knowledge to be, how we gain it, what we think we can do with it, and who we think has it will make a tremendous difference to future generations. The last decade of the 20th and the first decade of the 21st century have brought about major changes in the world's structure. Even as nations have become more globally interdependent and modes of communication so instantaneous that we can see and hear someone from across the Earth as a next-door neighbor, people are defining themselves by their differences—religious, economic, political, and ideological. Just as we have begun to need one another more than ever in mutual cooperation, just as our technologies permit us to better understand and collaborate with one another more productively, and just as poor nations and marginalized voices have begun to develop economically and gain a place in the world arena, there is a persistent fiber of mistrust and dissension that works against partnership and mutual progress.

CONSTRUCTIVE ENVISIONMENT BUILDING

From the envisionment-building perspective, the world's growth in technology, economic development, and communications has resulted from an

increase in knowledge and the ability to use that knowledge constructively and proactively. It grows from active envisionment-building minds that
are in motion, looking forward. It grows from flexible minds that know
how to cull and hone point-of-reference knowledge, but also know how
to approach the unfamiliar and explore horizons of possibilities. It grows
from the successful interplay of the two—critical and creative thought and
action.

Unfortunately, such growth is too often undermined by overdepen-
dence on existing ideas, concern with what we don't know, and the need
to fill in. This mind-set, different from the one that seeks knowledge
growth and is comfortable exploring new ideas, slows progress and miti-
gates against more dramatic gains. It holds us back as schools of learning,
as nations, and as fellow travelers in the world.

Educators and policymakers across the world are interested in the
contributions that higher-level critical and creative thinking can make
to knowledge growth. However, education in the disciplines has often
done little to teach them. Too often, critical thinking is presented as a
set of strategic activities that apply uniformly across disciplines, while
creative thinking is often considered the mark of a sloppy mind. I have
tried in this book to offer some concepts to move us forward, to offer a
pedagogical alternative that will permit students to learn their subject
matter more fully, to learn to think and communicate in ways that are
discipline-appropriate, and to learn to approach knowledge building in
more conceptually and pragmatically fulfilling ways—to become more
highly literate.

Further, I have shown that from an envisionment-building perspective,
students learn not only to understand disciplinary content, but to go beyond it, seeking understandings of links to real-world issues, examining
them critically and exploring new possibilities. In the world, as well as at
school, progress is neither continuous nor cumulative. It grows indirectly
as well as directly, through curiosity, searching, and reconnaissance, as
well as perseverance and critical analysis, within disciplines, across disciplines, and in life.

BUILDING KNOWLEDGE AND GAINING HIGHER LITERACY

To prepare them to become highly literate, students need opportunities
to experience disciplinary inquiry first-hand. They need to be cognitively

engaged in setting questions, exploring possibilities, developing points of reference, and finding ways to seek answers in all their coursework. They need to dig beneath the surface of the disciplines, to explore substantive issues and questions that they can connect to larger issues within the field and the world. They need to develop the habits of mind and the literacy abilities that will permit them to think, talk, read and write about, and use their knowledge flexibly, both in and out of school.

Schools remain sites where social as well as disciplinary conflicts can be confronted, and all students have a chance to participate constructively and grow. As shown in earlier chapters, all students, including struggling learners and those with special needs, can become engaged and learn in an envisionment-building classroom. So, too, do the highest-performing students, who are pushed to higher levels of understanding, knowledge building, and knowledge use. The nature of the activities in an envisionment-building classroom encourages all students to work at their level and, with teacher scaffolding and use of thought-provoking materials, move beyond.

Building knowledge involves multiple acts of envisionment building as we seek data and use them to go beyond the information given in ways that are discipline-appropriate, that work across disciplines, or that work in the real world. In this sense, knowledge is much deeper than simply getting information. Information counts, of course, but what we do with it, and to what end, creates knowledge. Gaining higher literacy in the academic disciplines involves learning the content, language, and ways of thinking and communicating that are considered signs of "knowing" within each discipline. It also involves being able to interact in interdisciplinary and real-world contexts, making the kinds of connections that are appropriate to advance thinking in those situations. It involves learning to read disciplinary and contextual codes and expectations and knowing how and when to use knowledge that will permit envisionments to continue to develop, in the range of settings we will encounter.

Although thoughtful reading, writing and discussion help build these habits of mind, technology can also be critically facilitative in supporting envisionment building (see, for example, Alverman, 2002; Gee, 2007; Rhodes & Robnolt, 2009; Scardamalia, 2006; Zhang, 2009). It can help students explore ideas, manipulate data, and try out paths and connections to see where they might lead. With technology, students can also build models, timelines, storyboards, concept maps, and other forms of representation, take them apart, and then reconfigure them.

TECHNOLOGY AS A
COGNITIVE PLAYGROUND FOR DISCIPLINARY LITERACY

From an envisionment-building perspective, the most productive and promising use of technology is its ability to provide students with cognitive "playgrounds" that let them take on disciplinary problems and manipulate ideas in thinking through their understandings and further developing them, with assistance from peers and teachers as well as the wider world. Online interactions with classmates as well as teachers are important opportunities for students to learn the vocabulary and modes of presentation and argument that are appropriate to the discipline. Uses of technology designed to involve students in working through problems as a way to understand how concepts, issues, and data interact and connect (or might connect) are available or being developed in every discipline. They are dramatically different from resources that function simply as data sources, although there is certainly a role for these, too. At the present time, however, web searches are by far the most frequently used purpose to which computers are put, aside from being used by students for word processing, PowerPoint presentations, and rote drill (Applebee & Langer, 2009).

Innovative teachers are also using blogs, text messaging, wikis, and other such formats to keep students interacting about the content they are learning in ways that give them ample opportunity to gain and give feedback, reflect on ideas, and gain practice in disciplinary literacy as their knowledge grows. New applications become available almost daily.

From an envisionment-building perspective, the most needed technology experiences—and those I have seen used least often—are the kind that let students manipulate and build from what they know around problems and issues in the disciplines and to think critically, creatively, and reflectively about them. Because technology is becoming the major worldwide mode in and through which people generate, reproduce, and communicate about knowledge, it must be included with reading, writing, and speaking as a tool for higher literacy across the disciplines. As a result, it must be given its place as a tool for knowledge building, learning, and communication in an envisionment-building classroom.

SUMMING UP

Overall, the goal of the envisionment-building classroom is to help students become better thinkers and knowers of the discipline, and to help them use their knowledge in productive, generative, and sometimes original ways. The habits of mind that students learn to develop in envisionment-building classrooms affect not only what they learn, but also how they go about learning both in school and out—for the moment and for the future.

As you have seen in the many classroom examples throughout this book, an envisionment-building approach improves how students pose and solve problems, consider connections, develop their understandings, and go beyond. This approach to gaining knowledge, as well as the particular knowledge that is gained, can also help students become more effective lifelong learners and more effective individuals—on the job, as family and community members, and as human beings.

> Logic takes you from A to B, creativity takes you everywhere.
> —Albert Einstein

> The two together make it all possible.
> —Judith Langer

References

Adler, M., & Rougle, A. (2005). *Building literacy through classroom discussion.* New York: Scholastic.

Alverman, D. E. (2002). *Adolescents and literacies in a digital world.* New York: Peter Lang.

Alverman, D. E., & Hagood, M. C. (2000). Critical media literacy: Research, theory and practice in new times. *Journal of Educational Research, 93*(3), 193–205.

Alvermann, D. E., Young, J. P., Weaver, D., Hinchman, K. A., Moore, D. W., Phelps, S. F., Thrash, E. C., & Zalewski, P. (1996). Middle and high school students' perceptions of how they experience text-based discussions: A multicase study. *Reading Research Quarterly, 31*(3), 244–267.

American Association for the Advancement of Science (AAAS). (1993). *Benchmarks for science literacy.* Retrieved March 18, 2010, from http://www.project2061.org/publications/bsl/default.htm

Applebee, A. N. (1996). *Curriculum as conversation.* Chicago: University of Chicago Press.

Applebee, A. N., & Langer, J. A. (2009). What's happening in the teaching of writing? *English Journal, 98*(5), 18–28.

Applebee, A. N., Langer, J. A., Nystrand, M., & Gamoran, A. (2003). Discussion-based approaches to developing understanding: Classroom instruction and student performance in middle and high school English. *American Educational Research Journal, 40*(3), 685–730.

Bakhtin, H. (1981). *The dialogic imagination.* Austin: University of Texas Press.

Bakhtin, M. (1986). *Speech genres and other late essays* (C. Emerson & M. Holquist, Trans.). Austin: University of Texas Press.

Beals, D. E., & Snow, C. E. (1994). Thunder is when the angels are upstairs bowling. *Narrative and Life History, 4*(4), 331–352.

Bissex, G. (1980). *Gnys at Wrk.* Cambridge, MA: Harvard University Press.

Bransford, J. D., & Donovan, S. D. (2005). Scientific inquiry and how people learn. In S. D. Donovan & J. D. Bransford, J.D. (Eds.), *How students learn: History, mathematics and science in the classroom* (pp. 397–419). Washington, DC: National Academies Press.

Britton, J. (1969). Talking to learn. In D. Barnes, J. Britton, & H. Rosen (Eds.), *Language, the learner and the school* (pp. 79–115). Harmondsworth, UK: Penguin.

Britton, J. (1970). *Language and learning*. London: Allen Lane-Penguin.

Brown, J. S., Collins, A., & Draguid, P. (1989). Situated cognition and the culture of learning. *Educational Researcher, 18*(1), 32–42.

Carpenter, T., Franke, M., & Levi, L. (2003). *Thinking mathematically*. Portsmouth, NH: Heinemann.

Carpenter, T. P., & Lehrer, R. (1999). Teaching and learning mathematics for understanding. In E. Fennema & T. A. Romberg (Eds.), *Mathematics classrooms that promote understanding* (pp. 19–35). Hillsdale, NJ: Erlbaum.

Chang-Wells, G. L., & Wells, G. (1992). *Constructing knowledge together*. Portsmouth, NH: Heinemann.

Close, E., Hull, M., & Langer, J. (2005). Writing and reading relationships in literacy learning. In R. Indrisano & J. R. Paratore (Eds.), *Learning to write, writing to learn: Theory and research in practice* (pp. 176–194). Newark, DE: International Reading Association.

Csikszentmihalyi, M. (1996). *Creativity: Flow and the psychology of discovery and invention*. New York: HarperCollins.

Dadie, B. (2001). La symbole. In S. R. Dietiker & D. van Hoof (Eds.), *En bonne forme* (pp. 18–20). Boston: Houghton Mifflin.

Donovan, S. D., & Bransford, J. D. (Eds.). (2005). *How students learn: History, mathematics and science in the classroom*. Washington, DC: National Academies Press.

Donovan, S. D., Wineburg, S., & Martin, D. (2004). Reading and rewriting history. *Educational Leadership, 62*(1), 42–46.

Dworkin, R. (1983). Law as interpretation. In W.J.T. Mitchell (Ed.), *The politics of interpretation* (pp. 271–286). Chicago: University of Chicago Press.

Elstein, A., Shulman, L., & Sprafka, S. (1978). *Medical problem-solving: The analysis of clinical reasoning*. Cambridge, MA: Harvard University Press.

Flood, J., Heath, S. B., & Lapp, D. (1997). *Handbook of research on teaching the communicative and visual arts*. New York: Macmillan.

Flood, J., Lapp, D., Brice-Heath, S. B., & Langer, J. A. (2009). The communicative, visual and performative arts: Core components of literacy education. In J. V. Hoffman & Y. M. Goodman (Eds.), *Changing literacies for changing times* (pp. 3–16). New York: Routledge.

Gambrell, L., & Almasi, J. (Eds.). (1996). *Lively discussions: Fostering engaged reading*. Newark, DE: International Reading Association.

Gardner, H. (2008). *Five minds for the future*. Boston: Harvard Business Press.

Gee, J. (2007). *What video games have to tell us about literacy learning* (2nd ed.). New York: Palgrave Macmillan.

Goodwin, D. K. (2005). *Team of rivals*. New York: Simon & Schuster.

Greenleaf, C. L., Schoenbach, R., Cziko, C., & Mueller, F. (2001). Apprenticing adolescent readers to academic literacy. *Harvard Educational Review, 71*(1), 70–127.

Groopman, J. (2007). *How doctors think*. New York: Houghton Mifflin.

Guthrie, J. T., & Wigfield, A. (2000). Engagement and motivation in reading. In M. L. Kamil, P. B. Mosenthal, P. D. Pearson, & R. Barr (Eds.), *Handbook of reading research* (Vol. III, pp. 403–422). New York: Erlbaum.

Gutierriez, K. (1993). How talk, context & script shape contexts for learning to write. *Linguistics and Education, 5*(3 & 4), 335–365.

Hakim, J. (2007). *A history of the U.S.* New York: Oxford University Press.

Kelly, D. L., Mullis, I.V.S., & Martin, M. O. (2000). *Profiles of student achievement in mathematics at the TIMSS international benchmarks: U.S. performance and standards in an international context*. Chestnut Hill, MA: International Study Center, Boston College.

Keys, C. W., Hand, B., Prain, V., & Collins, S. (1999). Using the science writing heuristic as a tool for learning from laboratory investigations in secondary science. *Journal of Research in Science Teaching, 36*(10), 1065–1084.

Koestler, A. (1964). *The act of creation: The study of the conscious and unconscious in science and art*. New York: Dell.

Kress, G., Jewitt, C., Franks, A., Hardcastle, J., Jones, K., & Bourne, J. (2005). *English in urban classrooms: A multicultural perspective on teaching and learning*. New York: Falmer.

Kuhn, T. (1962) *The structure of scientific revolutions*. Chicago: University of Chicago Press.

Langer, J. A. (1985). What eight-year-olds know about expository writing. *Educational Perspectives, 23*(3), 27–33.

Langer, J. A. (1986a). *Children reading & writing*. Norwood, NJ: Ablex.

Langer, J. A. (1986b). Learning through writing: Study skills in the content areas. *Journal of Reading, 29*(5), 401–406.

Langer, J. A. (1987). A sociocognitive perspective on literacy. In J. Langer (Ed.), *Language, literacy and culture: Issues of society and schooling* (pp. 1–20). Norwood, NJ: Ablex.

Langer, J. A. (1990). The process of understanding: Reading for literary and informational purposes. *Research in the Teaching of English, 24*(3), 229–260.

Langer, J. A. (1992a). Speaking of knowing: Conceptions of understanding in academic disciplines. In A. Herrington & C. Moran (Eds.), *Writing, teaching and learning in the disciplines* (pp. 69–85). New York: Modern Language Association.

Langer, J. A. (1992b). *Academic learning and critical reasoning: A study of knowing in the academic subjects* [Final report to the U.S. Department of Education, Grant No. R117E0051]. Washington, DC: Office of Educational Research and Improvement.

Langer, J. A. (1994). Teaching disciplinary thinking in academic coursework. In J. N. Mangieri & C. Collins (Eds.), *Advanced educational psychology: Creating effective schools and powerful thinkers* (pp. 82–109). New York: Harcourt, Brace, Jovanovich.

Langer, J. A. (1995). *Envisioning literature: Literary understanding and literature instruction.* New York: Teachers College Press.

Langer, J. A. (2001). Beating the odds: Teaching middle and high school students to read and write well. *American Educational Research Journal, 38*(4), 837–880.

Langer, J. A. (2004). *Getting to excellent.* New York: Teachers College Press.

Langer, J. A. (2008). Contexts for adolescent literacy. In L. Christenbury, R. Bomer, & P. Smagorinsky (Eds.), *Handbook of adolescent literacy* (pp. 49–64). New York: Guilford Press.

Langer, J. A. (2010). *Envisioning literature: Literary understanding and literature instruction* (2nd ed.). New York: Teachers College Press.

Langer, J. A., & Applebee, A. N. (1987). *How writing shapes thinking.* Urbana, IL: National Council of Teachers of English.

Langer, J. A., & Applebee, A. N. (1988). *Speaking of knowing* [Final Report to the U.S. Department of Education, Grant No. G0086110967]. Washington, DC: Office of Research and Improvement.

Langer, J. A., Applebee, A. N., & Nystrand, M. (2005, May). The partnership for literacy. In J. A. Langer, A. N. Applebee, & M. Nystrand, *National Research Center on English Learning and Achievement* [Final Report to the Institute for Educational Sciences, Washington, D.C. Grant #R305960005] (pp. 52–102). Albany, NY: National Research Center on English Learning and Achievement.

Langer, S. (1942). *Philosophy in a new key.* Cambridge, MA: Harvard University Press.

Latour, B. (1990). *Science in action.* Cambridge, MA: Harvard University Press

Lee, C. D. (2007). *Culture, literacy and learning: Taking bloom in the midst of the whirlwind.* New York: Teachers College Press.

Lee, P. J. (2005). Putting principles into practice: Understanding history. In S. D. Donovan & J. D. Bransford (Eds.), *How students learn: History, mathematics and science in the classroom* (pp. 31–78). Washington, DC: National Academies Press.

Lehrer, R., Carpenter, S., Schauble, L., & Putz, A. (2000). Designing classrooms that support inquiry. In J. Minstrell & E. van Zee (Eds.), *Inquiring into inquiry learning and teaching in science* (pp. 80–99). Washington, DC: American Association for the Advancement of Science.

Lemke, J. L. (1990). *Talking science: Language learning and values.* Norwood, NJ: Ablex.

Liberg, C., Espmark, L., Wiksten, J., & Butler, I. (1997). *Observations, recounts, narratives and language learning.* Uppsala, Sweden: Uppsala University Department of Linguistics.

Macrorie, K. (1988). *The I-search paper.* Portsmouth, NH: Boynton Cook/Heinemann.

McCommas, W. F. (1996). Ten myths of science: Re-examining what we think we know about the nature of science. *School Science and Mathematics, 96*(1), 10–16.

Morris, C. W. (1971). *Writing on the general theory of signs.* The Hague: Mouton.

National Council of Teachers of English & International Reading Association. (2009). *NCTE/IRA standards for the English language arts*. Retrieved March 23, 2010, from http://www.ncte.org/positions

New London Group. (1987). A pedagogy of multiliteracies: Designing social futures. *Harvard Educational Review, 66*(1), 60–92.

Nystrand, N. (1997). *Opening dialogue*. New York: Teachers College Press.

Obama, B. (1995). *Dreams from my father*. New York: Three Rivers Press.

Orr, J. E. (1987, June). Narratives at work: Storytelling as cooperative diagnostic activity. *Field Service Manager: The Journal of Field Service Managers International, 11*(6), 47–60.

Pappas, C. C. (1991). Fostering full access to literacy by including information books. *Language Arts, 68*(6), 449–462.

Peirce, C. S. (1992). *The essential Peirce: Selected philosophical writings. Vol. 1, 1867–1893*. Bloomington: Indiana University Press.

Pressley, M., Allington, R. L., Wharton-McDonald, R., Block, C. C., & Morrow, L. M. (2001). *Learning to read: Lessons from exemplary first grade classrooms*. New York: Guilford Press.

Renne, J. (2009, February). A molecular checkup. *Scientific American, 3000*(2), 8.

Rhodes, J. A., & Robnolt, V. J. (2009). Digital literacies in the classroom. In L. Christenbury, R. Bomer, & P. Smagorinsky (Eds.), *Handbook of adolescent literacy research* (pp. 153–169). New York: Guilford Press.

Rodgers, C. (2002, Summer). Seeing student learning: Teacher change and the role of reflection. *Harvard Educational Review, 72*(2), 230–253.

Romberg, T. A., & Kaput, J. J. (1999). Mathematics worth teaching, mathematics worth understanding. In E. Fennema & T. A. Romberg (Eds.), *Mathematics classrooms that promote understanding* (pp. 3–19). Hillsdale, NJ: Erlbaum.

Rosenblatt, L. (1978). *The reader, the text, the poem*. Cambridge, MA: Harvard University Press. (Original work published 1938)

Sakai, K. (1990). *Sachiko means happiness*. San Francisco: Children's Book Press.

Scardamalia, M. (2006). Technology for understanding. In K. Leithwood, P. McAdie, N. Bascia, & A. Rodriguez (Eds.), *Teaching for deep understanding: What every educator needs to know* (pp. 103–109). Thousand Oaks, CA: Corwin.

Schauble, L. (1996). Building functional models: Designing an elbow. *Journal of Research in Science Teaching, 34*(2), 125–143.

Schifter, D. (Ed.). (1996). *What's happening in math class?* (Vol. 1). New York: Teachers College Press.

Sebeok, T. A., & Danesi, M. (2000). *The forms of meaning: Modeling systems theory and semiotic analysis*. Berlin: Mouton de Gruyter.

Shanahan, T., & Shanahan C. (2008). Teaching disciplinary literacy to adolescents: Rethinking content-area literacy. *Harvard Education Review, 78*(1), 40–59.

Sternberg, R. J., Grigorenko, E. L., & Singer, J. L. (Eds.). (2004). *Creativity: From potential to realization*. Washington, DC: American Psychological Association.

Willingham, D. T. (2007). Critical thinking: Why is it so hard to teach? *American Educator* (Summer), 8–19.

Willinsky, J. (1990). *The new literacy: Redefining reading and writing in schools.* New York: Routledge.

Wineburg, S. (1994). Out of our past and into our future: The psychological study of learning and teaching history. *Educational Psychologist, 29*(2), 57–60.

Wineburg, S. (2005). What does NCATE have to say to future history teachers? Not much. *Phi Delta Kappan, 86*(9), 658–665.

Wineburg, S. (2007). Unnatural and essential: The nature of historical thinking. *Teaching History, 129*(December), 6–11.

Yackel, E., & Cobb, P. (1996). Sociomathematical norms, argumentation and autonomy in mathematics. *Journal for Research in Mathematics Education, 27*(4), 458–477.

Yolen, J. (1992). *Encounter.* New York: Harcourt Brace.

Zecker, L. B. (1996). Early development in written language: Children's emergent knowledge of genre-specific characteristics. *Journal of Reading and Writing, 8*(1), 5–25.

Zhang, J. (2009). Towards a creative social web for learners and teachers. *Educational Researcher, 38*(May), 274–279.

Index

Academic knowledge. *See also specific disciplines*
  enculturation into an academic discipline, 53
  from home to school, 4–8
  during school years, 8–11
Academic literacy, 2–12
  defined, 2
  disciplinary thought and knowledge and, 3
  expository form, 3–4, 5–6
  growth of, 3–11
  importance of, 11–12
Ackley, David, 131, 134, 143–145
Adler, M., 37, 132
Alcott, Louisa May, 122–124
Allington, R. L., 115
Almasi, J., 115
Alverman, D. E., 115, 117, 157
American Association for the Advancement of Science (AAAS), 78
Annotations of text, 37, 144
Applebee, Arthur N., 43, 54, 77, 116, 133, 158
Apprenticing students, 77–78

Bakhtin, H., 116
Beals, D. E., 3
Bergman, Ingmar, 36

Bias focus, 55
Big conversations and connected concepts, 45–47
Big ideas, 57–58
Biology, knowledge in, 1
Bissex, G., 3
Blackboard, 137
Block, C., 115
Book reports, 7, 8
Border Problem, 146–148
Bourne, J., 12
Brainstorming, 97
Branchtree Middle School, 46–47
Bransford, J. D., 55, 78
Brice-Heath, S. B., 13
Britton, James, 116
Brooks, Arthea, 44–45
Brown, John Seely, 27 n. 1, 78
Butler, I., 3, 5

Carpenter, S., 78
Carpenter, T. P., 92, 94
Carroll, Laura, 67–73, 75, 126–129
Chang-Wells, G. L., 115–116
Channing, Ellery, 122–124
Close, E., 115
Clustering activities, 144
Cobb, P., 94
Collins, A., 78
Collins, S., 82

Communities of inquiry. *See also* Professional community
  envisionment-building classrooms as, 41
Comparisons and analysis of evidence, 55
  literary comparisons, 120–121
  scientific knowledge, 78–80
Content areas. *See* Disciplinary thought and knowledge
Context focus, 55
Cory, Meg, 50
Critical thinking
  within disciplines, 42–43, 61, 88–90, 103, 116, 139–142, 145
  in envisionment-building classrooms, 41–42
  in Envisionment-Building Guides, 26
  levels of, 142
  professional community, 151–153
  stances and, 26, 55, 56, 69–70, 89, 90, 99–100, 103
  surveying students on, 139–142
  "ways to think" strategies and, 49–50, 58, 74
Csikszentmihalyi, M., 36
CultureGrams, 67–68, 70–73
Curriculum, forging connections in, 45–47, 58–59
Cziko, C., 78

Dadie, Bernard, 39
Danesi, M., 12
Dialogue, in early literacy, 4–5
Disciplinary thought and knowledge. *See also specific disciplines*
  constructive envisionment building, 155–156
  enculturation, 53
  gaining higher literacy, 156–157
  literacy in, 155–159

technology as cognitive playground, 158
  thinking within disciplines, 42–43
Discussion
  critical thinking and, 140–141
  professional community, 136–137
  substantive and sustained discussion and writing, 47–49, 80–88, 94–103
Discussion guides, 37
Donovan, S. D., 55, 78
Draguid, P., 78
Dramatic play, 4–5
Dreams from My Father (Obama), 13–14, 17–18
Dworkin, R., 33

Early literacy, 4–8
  dialogue, 4–5
  dramatic play, 4–5
Earth science, envisionment-building classrooms, 49
Einstein, Albert, 159
Elstein, A., 33
Emerson, Ralph Waldo, 122, 124, 125
Enabling strategies, in minds-on teaching, 49–50
Encounter (Yolen), 58–59
English
  cognitive and linguistic aspects of, 115–117
  critical thinking in, 140
  envisionment building in, 44–45, 50, 114–130
  horizons of possibilities thinking, 44–45, 115, 125–126, 129
  literary comparisons, 121–126
  minds-on teaching, 117
  online research, 126–129
  point of reference thinking, 44–45, 115, 125–126, 129
  thinking with and through language, 114–115

vocabulary and content exploration, 117–121
writing about literature, 116, 125–126
Envisagements, 27 n. 1
Envisionment, introduction to concept, 27 n. 1
Envisionment building, 16–27. *See also* Envisionment-building classrooms
knowledge development as envisionment building, 17–18, 155–159
literacy in disciplinary knowledge, 155–156
in minds-on teaching, 43–45
nature of envisionment, 16–17, 18–19
in professional communities, 131–154
stances during, 21–23
Envisionment-building classrooms, 39–52. *See also* Envisionment building
communities of inquiry in, 41
critical-thinking strategies, 41–42
English, 44–45, 50, 114–130
individual within the group, 51
mathematics, 19–21, 92–113
minds-on teaching in, 43–50
science, 34–35, 47–49, 77–91
social studies/history, 24–27, 36–38, 44–45, 46–47, 53–76
thinking within a discipline, 42–43
Envisionment-Building Guides, 24–27
critical thinking about material, 26
developing understanding of material, 25
getting started with material, 24–25
going beyond material, 26–27
learning from material, 25, 55, 72 ·
nature of, 24
in social studies/history, 24–27
Espmark, L., 3, 5
Expository knowledge, 3–4, 5–6

Farina, Laurie, 131, 132, 137, 150–152
Fillmore, Charles, 27 n. 1
Flood, J., 13, 117
Franke, M., 94
Franks, A., 12
Frost, David, 13–14
Frost/Nixon (Frost), 13–14

Gambrell, L., 115
Gamoran, A., 43, 116
Gardner, H., 36
Gee, J., 116, 117, 157
Getting to Excellent (Langer), 154
Goodwin, Doris Kearns, 17–18, 21–22
Great Global Warming Swindle, The (film), 88–89
Greenleaf, C. L., 78
Grigorenko, E. L., 36
Groopman, Jerome, 33
Gutenberg, Johannes, 34–36
Guthrie, J. T., 115
Gutierriez, K., 116

Hagood, M. C., 115, 117
Hakim, Joy, 58
Hand, B., 82
Hardcastle, J., 12
Harris, Andres, 88–90
Heath, S. B., 117
Hidden features of language, 114–115
Hinchman, K. A., 115
History of the U.S., A (Hakim), 58
Horizons of possibilities thinking
English examples, 44–45, 115, 125–126, 129
goal of, 32
impact on instruction, 30–32
nature of orientation, 29–30
questions in, 31
relationship to point of reference thinking, 32–35
science examples, 34–35, 80–88, 103

Horizons of possibilities thinking
(*continued*)
  social studies/history examples,
    36–38, 44–45, 46–47
Hull, M., 115

Idea Catcher, 68–70, 126–129
Inconvenient Truth, An (film), 88–89
Individual within the group, 51
Informational experiences, 2
Instructional tools
  features of minds-on teaching, 43–50
  stances as, 23–27
Interactive learning environment, 143
International Reading Association
    (IRA), 114
I-search activity, 150–151

Jewitt, C., 12
Jones, K., 12
Jones, Ken, 48–49
Journal writing, student, 6–7
Judd, Monica, 80–88, 90, 131

Kaput, J. J., 92, 93
Kay, Paul, 27 n. 1
Kelly, D. L., 92
Keys, C. W., 82
Knowledge
  nature of, 1
  as relational, 1–2
Knowledge development, as
    envisionment building, 17–18,
    155–159
Koestler, Arthur, 33–36
Kress, G., 12
Kuhn, T., 36

Lab reports, 8–11
Langer, Judith A., 2, 3–4, 12, 13, 22, 27
    n. 1, 28, 30, 42, 43, 48, 54, 55, 77, 78,
    115, 116, 130, 132, 133, 152–153, 154,
    158, 159

Langer, Suzanne, 27 n. 1
Lapp, D., 13, 117
Latour, B., 78
"Learning to do" strategies, 50
"Learning to think" strategies, 50
Lee, C. D., 115, 116–117
Lee, P. J., 56
Lehrer, R., 78, 92
Lemke, J. L., 78
Levi, L., 94
Liberg, C., 3, 5
Lincoln, Abraham, 17–18, 21
Literacy goals, professional
    community, 149–150
Literary stories, 7
Literate knowledge, 28–38. *See also*
    Horizons of possibilities thinking;
    Point of reference thinking
  fostering both orientations in
    disciplinary classes, 36–38
  impact of orientations on instruction,
    30–32
  orientations relating to one another,
    32–35
  orientations toward meaning, 28–30
  role in disciplines, 155–159
Literate thinking, 12–14
Little Men (Alcott), 123
Little Women (Alcott), 122

Macrorie, K., 150
Martin, D., 55
Martin, M. O., 92
Massina, Tony, 19–22
Mathematics, 7
  critical thinking in, 140
  developing math concepts through
    problem-based activities, 103–112
  enabling strategies in, 49–50
  envisionment building in, 19–21,
    92–113
  learning by engaging in applied
    activities, 92–94

minds-on teaching, 112
problem-solving in, 95–96, 103–112
ratios, 110–112
rubrics in, 109, 113
stances in, 97–102
sustained discussion and problem
    solving in, 94–103
writing in, 94–103, 104–110, 145–148
McCommas, W. F., 79
Meaning, orientations toward, 28–30
Metacognitive reflection, 151–152
Minds-on teaching, 43–50
    building envisionments, 43–45
    enabling strategies, 49–50
    English, 117
    forging curricular connections,
        45–47, 58–59
    mathematics, 112
    nature of, 41
    science, 79, 102–103
    social studies/history, 57–67, 73–75
    substantive and sustained discussion
        and writing, 47–49, 80–88, 94–103
Monteiro, Cara, 36–38
Moore, D. W., 115
Morris, C. W., 12
Morrow, L. M., 115
Motivation focus, 55
Mueller, F., 78
Mullis, I. V. S., 92
Mutford, Jason, 94–103, 112

National Assessment of Educational
    Progress (NAEP), xi–xii
National Council of Teachers of
    English (NCTE), 114
National Research Center in Mathe-
    matical Sciences Education, 92
New London Group, 115
New Yorker, 33
Nixon, Richard, 13
Nonverbal cues, 6
Nystrand, Martin, 43, 47, 116, 133

Obama, Barack, 13, 17–18, 21
Online discussions, in social studies/
    history, 70–73
Online research, English, 126–129
Open mind diagrams, 37
Orr, J. E., 33

Pappas, C. C., 3
Parallelograms, 96
Partnership for Literacy (P4L), 46–47,
    133–134, 142
Peirce, C. S., 12
Persuasive essays, 44–45
Phelps, S. F., 115
Physics
    critical thinking in, 88–90
    knowledge in, 1–2
    substantive and sustained discussion
        and writing in, 47–49
Play, dramatic, 4–5
Poe, Edgar Allan, 123
Point of reference thinking
    English examples, 44–45, 115, 125–
        126, 129
    goal of, 32
    impact on instruction, 30–32
    nature of orientation, 29
    questions in, 31
    relationship to horizons of
        possibilities thinking, 32–35
    science examples, 34–35, 79, 80–88, 103
    social studies/history examples,
        36–38, 44–45, 46–47, 73
Poking around, in envisionment
    building, 22
Polsinelli, Karen, 57–67, 72, 75, 143
Prain, V., 82
Pressley, M., 115
Printing press, 34–35
Problem-solving
    in mathematics, 95–96, 103–112
    in professional communities, 135–137
    in science, 77–78, 93–94

Professional community, 131–154
  continuing self-study, 151–153
  discussion guidelines, 136–137
  enacting, 142–148
  extended I-search activity, 150–151
  learning and thinking in disciplines,
    148–151
  learning goals, 132
  literacy goals, 149–150
  planning, 138–142, 148
  problem-based, minds-on activities,
    135–137
  reflection, 137–138
  summer retreat, 134–135
  Team 82, 131–154
  technology incorporation, 137
Putz, A., 78

Questions, in point of reference
    thinking, 31
Quickwrites, 44

Ratios, 110–112
Reasoning abilities, 12–14
Recounting, 7
Renne, J., 19
Rhodes, J. A., 117, 157
Robnolt, V. J., 117, 157
Rock Shake Experiment, 8–11
Rodgers, C., 142
Roeser, Randall, 50, 103–112, 131, 134,
    138, 145–148
Romberg, T. A., 92, 93
Rosales, Ella, 117–121
Rosales, John, 44–45
Rosenblatt, L., 115
Rougle, A., 37, 132
Rougle, Eija, 46–47, 134–136, 142, 148
Round-robin reading, 40
Rubrics
  in mathematics, 109, 113
  in social studies/history, 65, 66, 73–74

Sachiko Means Happiness (Sakai),
    126–129
Sakai, Kimiko, 126–129
Saraband (film), 30
Scardamalia, M., 116, 157
Schauble, L., 78
Schifter, D., 94
Schoenbach, R., 78
School learning, 3–4
School talk, 7
Science
  apprenticing students, 77–78
  critical thinking in, 88–90, 139–140
  envisionment-building classrooms,
    34–35, 47–49, 77–91
  horizons of possibilities thinking,
    34–35, 80–88, 103
  lab reports, 8–11
  language and content focus in,
    83–86
  minds-on teaching, 79, 102–103
  nature of scientific knowledge,
    78–80
  nature of student learning, 88
  point of reference thinking, 34–35, 79,
    80–88, 103
  problem-solving, 77–78, 93–94
  shifts in attention, 33–34
  Soda Can Experiment, 80–86
  stances in, 88–90
  states of matter and, 87–88
  sustained discussion and writing
    about experiments, 47–49, 80–88
  writing in, 47–49, 80–88
Scientific American, 19
Sebeok, T. A., 12
Shanahan, C., 55, 78
Shanahan, T., 55, 78
Shulman, L., 33
Singer, J. L., 36
SMART Boards, 39–40, 104
Snow, C. E., 3

Snyder, Mrs., 73–75
Social studies/history
  critical thinking in, 139
  curricular connections in, 46–47,
    58–59
  enculturation into an academic
    discipline, 53
  Envisionment-Building Guides in,
    24–27
  envisionment building in, 24–27,
    36–38, 44–45, 46–47, 53–76
  explicit thinking in, 59–65
  horizons of possibilities thinking,
    36–38, 44–45, 46–47
  insider's look at, 54
  instructional foci in, 55–57
  knowledge in, 1
  manipulation of content in, 54
  minds-on social studies/history
    class, 57–67, 73–75
  nature of student learning in, 65–67
  online discussion in, 73–75
  point of reference thinking, 36–38,
    44–45, 46–47, 73
  research on the Web, 70–73
  rubrics in, 65, 66, 73–74
  stances in, 55–57, 67–73
  variety of disciplines in, 56
  writing in, 54, 143–145
Soda Can Experiment, 80–86
Source evaluation, 55
Sprafka, S., 33
Stances
  being in and moving through
    envisionment, 22
  being out and stepping into
    envisionment, 22
  critical thinking about material, 26,
    55, 56, 69–70, 89, 90, 99–100, 103
  developing understanding of
    material, 25, 55, 56, 69–70, 72, 90,
    98–99, 103, 105–107
  during envisionment building, 21–23
  getting started with material, 24–25,
    69–70, 72, 90, 97–98, 103, 104–105
  going beyond material, 26–27, 56, 70
  as instructional tool, 23–27
  learning from material, 25, 55, 72
  leaving an envisionment and going
    beyond, 23
  in mathematics, 97–102
  nature of, 22
  in science, 88–90
  in social studies/history, 55–57,
    67–73
  stepping out and objectifying the
    experience, 23
  stepping out and rethinking what
    you know, 23
"Stand and Deliver" activities, 37, 144
Sternberg, R. J., 36
Subject-area disciplines. *See*
    Disciplinary thought and
    knowledge *and specific disciplines*
Substantive and sustained discussion
    and writing, 94–103
  in mathematics, 94–103
  in science, 47–49, 80–88
"Le Symbole" (Dadie), 39

Tan, Amy, 50
T-charts, 44
Team 82, 131–154
  beginning of collaborative project,
    133–134
  described, 131
  discussion guidelines, 136–137
  Partnership for Literacy (P4L), 46–47,
    133–134, 142
  planning, 138–142
  reflecting, 137–138
  summer retreat, 134–135
Team of Rivals (Goodwin), 17–18,
    21–22

Technology
  as cognitive playground for
    disciplinary literacy, 158
  professional community, 137
Text annotations, 37, 144
Think Charts, 61–63, 141
Third International Mathematics and
  Science Study (TIMSS), 92
Thoreau, Henry David, 122, 123, 125
Thrash, E. C., 115
Twain, Mark, 117

Vocabulary development, 117–121
  exploring text, 120–121
  exploring word meaning, 118–120

"Ways to do" strategies, 49–50, 58, 65
"Ways to think" strategies, 49–50, 58,
  74
Weaver, D., 115
Web-based research/discussion, in
  social studies/history, 70–75
Wells, G., 115–116
Wharton-McDonald, R., 115
Wigfield, A., 115

Wiksten, J., 3, 5
Willingham, D. T., 138
Willinsky, J., 116–117
Wineburg, Sam, 53, 55
Word problems, 7
Wright, Denise, 121–126
Writing
  critical thinking and, 141
  in English, 116, 125–126
  in mathematics, 94–103, 104–110,
    145–148
  in science, 47–49, 80–88
  in social studies/history, 54,
    143–145
  substantive and sustained discussion
    and writing, 47–49, 80–88, 94–103

Yackel, E., 94
Yolen, Jane, 58
Young, J. P., 115

Zalewski, P., 115
Zank, George, 49, 50
Zecker, L. B., 3
Zhang, J., 116, 157

About the Author

Judith A. Langer is Distinguished Professor at the University at Albany, State University of New York, where she is founder and director of the Albany Institute for Research in Education and director of the National Research Center on English Learning and Achievement. She is an internationally known scholar in literacy education. Her research focuses on how people become highly literate; on how they use reading, writing, and language to learn; and on what this means for instruction. Langer's work has had a strong international and national impact on policy and practice as well as theory.

Author of numerous research reports, articles, chapters, and monographs, she has written 11 books. Her latest, *Envisioning Literature: Literary Understanding and Literature Instruction*, Second Edition, was just released by Teachers College Press, along with *Envisioning Knowledge: Building Literacy in the Academic Disciplines*.

Langer sits on six editorial boards and has reviewed for 17 national and international journals. She has received several notable awards, among them an honorary doctorate from the University of Uppsala, Sweden; the Imaginative Scientists of the World award from Lund University, Sweden; distinguished Benton Fellow, University of Chicago; Fellow and Scholar-in-Residence, Rockefeller Foundation, Bellagio, Italy; distinguished Visiting Scholar, University of Turku (Finland); Chancellor's Award for Exemplary Contributions to Research, and Presidential Award for Lifetime Achievement, Hofstra University. She has also been inducted into the International Reading Hall of Fame and received the Albert J. Harris award for research on teaching students with reading difficulties.